Mary K. Bauer
500 Harvard St
Mpls 14
Feb. '62

Poems 1923-1954

E. E. CUMMINGS

Poems

1923-1954

HARCOURT, BRACE AND COMPANY · NEW YORK

To Marion

Contents

Tulips and Chimneys (1923)

CHIMNEYS

& [AND] (1925)

XLI POEMS (1925)

SONGS

is 5 (1926)

W [ViVa] (1931)

no thanks (1935)

New Poems [from Collected Poems] (1938)

50 POEMS (1940)

1 x 1 [One Times One] (1944)

1

x

XAIPE (1950)

Tulips and Chimneys

Tulips

EPITHALAMION

I.

Thou aged unreluctant earth who dost
with quivering continual thighs invite
the thrilling rain the slender paramour
to toy with thy extraordinary lust,
(the sinuous rain which rising from thy bed
steals to his wife the sky and hour by hour
wholly renews her pale flesh with delight)
—immortally whence are the high gods fled?

Speak elm eloquent pandar with thy nod
significant to the ecstatic earth
in token of his coming whom her soul
burns to embrace—and didst thou know the god
from but the imprint of whose cloven feet
the shrieking dryad sought her leafy goal,
at the mere echo of whose shining mirth
the furious hearts of mountains ceased to beat?

Wind beautifully who wanderest
over smooth pages of forgotten joy
proving the peaceful theorems of the flowers
—didst e'er depart upon more exquisite quest?
and did thy fortunate fingers sometime dwell
(within a greener shadow of secret bowers)
among the curves of that delicious boy
whose serious grace one goddess loved too well?

Chryselephantine Zeus Olympian
sceptred colossus of the Pheidian soul
whose eagle frights creation, in whose palm
Nike presents the crown sweetest to man,
whose lilied robe the sun's white hands emboss,
betwixt whose absolute feet anoint with calm
of intent stars circling the acerb pole
poises, smiling, the diadumenos

in whose young chiseled eyes the people saw
their once again victorious Pantarkes
(whose grace the prince of artists made him bold
to imitate between the feet of awe),
thunderer whose omnipotent brow showers
its curls of unendured eternal gold
over the infinite breast in bright degrees,
whose pillow is the graces and the hours,

father of gods and men whose subtle throne
twain sphinxes bear each with a writhing youth
caught to her brazen breasts, whose foot-stool tells
how fought the looser of the warlike zone
of her that brought forth tall Hippolytus,
lord on whose pedestal the deep expels
(over Selene's car closing uncouth)
of Helios the sweet wheels tremulous—

are there no kings in Argos, that the song
is silent, of the steep unspeaking tower
within whose brightening strictness Danæ
saw the night severed and the glowing throng
descend, felt on her flesh the amorous strain
of gradual hands and yielding to that fee
her eager body's unimmortal flower
knew in the darkness a more burning rain?

2.

And still the mad magnificent herald Spring
assembles beauty from forgetfulness
with the wild trump of April: witchery
of sound and odour drives the wingless thing
man forth into bright air, for now the red
leaps in the maple's cheek, and suddenly
by shining hordes in sweet unserious dress
ascends the golden crocus from the dead.

On dappled dawn forth rides the pungent sun
with hooded day preening upon his hand
followed by gay untimid final flowers
(which dressed in various tremulous armor stun
the eyes of ragged earth who sees them pass)
while hunted from his kingdom winter cowers,
seeing green armies steadily expand
hearing the spear-song of the marching grass.

A silver sudden parody of snow
tickles the air to golden tears, and hark!
the flicker's laughing yet, while on the hills
the pines deepen to whispers primeval and throw
backward their foreheads to the barbarous bright
sky, and suddenly from the valley thrills
the unimaginable upward lark
and drowns the earth and passes into light

(slowly in life's serene perpetual round
a pale world gathers comfort to her soul,
hope richly scattered by the abundant sun
invades the new mosaic of the ground
—let but the incurious curtaining dusk be drawn
surpassing nets are sedulously spun
to snare the brutal dew,—the authentic scroll
of fairie hands and vanishing with dawn).

Spring, that omits no mention of desire
in every curved and curling thing, yet holds
continuous intercourse—through skies and trees
the lilac's smoke the poppy's pompous fire
the pansy's purple patience and the grave
frailty of daisies—by what rare unease
revealed of teasingly transparent folds—
with man's poor soul superlatively brave.

Surely from robes of particoloured peace
with mouth flower-faint and undiscovered eyes
and dim slow perfect body amorous
(whiter than lilies which are born and cease
for being whiter than this world) exhales
the hovering high perfume curious
of that one month for whom the whole year dies,
risen at length from palpitating veils.

O still miraculous May! O shining girl
of time untarnished! O small intimate
gently primeval hands, frivolous feet
divine! O singular and breathless pearl!
O indefinable frail ultimate pose!
O visible beatitude sweet sweet
intolerable! silence immaculate
of god's evasive audible great rose!

3.

Lover, lead forth thy love unto that bed
prepared by whitest hands of waiting years,
curtained with wordless worship absolute,
unto the certain altar at whose head
stands that clear candle whose expecting breath
exults upon the tongue of flame half-mute,
(haste ere some thrush with silver several tears
complete the perfumed paraphrase of death).

Now is the time when all occasional things
close into silence, only one tree, one
svelte translation of eternity
unto the pale meaning of heaven clings,
(whose million leaves in winsome indolence
simmer upon thinking twilight momently)
as down the oblivious west's numerous dun
magnificence conquers magnificence.

In heaven's intolerable athanor
inimitably tortured the base day
utters at length her soft intrinsic hour,
and from those tenuous fires which more and more
sink and are lost the divine alchemist,
the magus of creation, lifts a flower—
whence is the world's insufferable clay
clothed with incognizable amethyst.

Lady at whose imperishable smile
the amazed doves flicker upon sunny wings
as if in terror of eternity,
(or seeming that they would mistrust a while
the moving of beauteous dead mouths throughout
that very proud transparent company
of quivering ghosts-of-love which scarcely sings
drifting in slow diaphanous faint rout),

queen in the inconceivable embrace
of whose tremendous hair that blossom stands
whereof is most desire, yet less than those
twain perfect roses whose ambrosial grace,
goddess, thy crippled thunder-forging groom
or the loud lord of skipping mænads knows,—
having Discordia's apple in thy hands,
which the scared shepherd gave thee for his doom—

O thou within the chancel of whose charms
the tall boy god of everlasting war
received the shuddering sacrament of sleep,
betwixt whose cool incorrigible arms
impaled upon delicious mystery,
with gaunt limbs reeking of the whispered deep,
deliberate groping ocean fondled o'er
the warm long flower of unchastity,

imperial Cytherea, from frail foam
sprung with irrevocable nakedness
to strike the young world into smoking song—
as the first star perfects the sensual dome
of darkness, and the sweet strong final bird
transcends the sight, O thou to whom belong
the hearts of lovers!—I beseech thee bless
thy suppliant singer and his wandering word.

OF NICOLETTE

dreaming in marble all the castle lay
like some gigantic ghost-flower born of night
blossoming in white towers to the moon,
soft sighed the passionate darkness to the tune
of tiny troubadours, and (phantom-white)
dumb-blooming boughs let fall their glorious snows,
and the unearthly sweetness of a rose
swam upward from the troubled heart of May;

a Winged Passion woke and one by one
there fell upon the night, like angel's tears,
the syllables of that mysterious prayer,
and as an opening lily drowsy-fair
(when from her couch of poppy petals peers
the sleepy morning) gently draws apart
her curtains, and lays bare her trembling heart
with beads of dew made jewels by the sun,

so one high shining tower (which as a glass
turned light to flame and blazed with snowy fire)
unfolding, gave the moon a nymphlike face,
a form whose snowy symmetry of grace
haunted the limbs as music haunts the lyre,
a creature of white hands, who letting fall
a thread of lustre from the castle wall
glided, a drop of radiance, to the grass—

shunning the sudden moonbeam's treacherous snare
she sought the harbouring dark, and (catching up
her delicate silk) all white, with shining feet,
went forth into the dew: right wildly beat
her heart at every kiss of daisy-cup,
and from her cheek the beauteous colour went
with every bough that reverently bent
to touch the yellow wonder of her hair.

SONGS

I

(thee will i praise between those rivers whose
white voices pass upon forgetting (fail
me not) whose courseless waters are a gloat
of silver; o'er whose night three willows wail,
a slender dimness in the unshapeful hour
making dear moan in tones of stroked flower;
let not thy lust one threaded moment lose:
haste) the very shadowy sheep float
free upon terrific pastures pale,

whose tall mysterious shepherd lifts a cheek
teartroubled to the momentary wind
with guiding smile, lips wisely minced for blown
kisses, condemnatory fingers thinned
of pity—so he stands counting the moved
myriads wonderfully loved,
(hasten, it is the moment which shall seek
all blossoms that do learn, scents of not known
musics in whose careful eyes are dinned;

and the people of perfect darkness fills
his mind who will their hungering whispers hear
with weepings soundless, saying of "alas
we were chaste on earth we ghosts: hark to the sheer
cadence of our gray flesh in the gloom!
and still to be immortal is our doom;
but a rain frailly raging whom the hills
sink into and their sunsets, it shall pass.
Our feet tread sleepless meadows sweet with fear")

then be with me: unseriously seem
by the perusing greenness of thy thought
my golden soul fabulously to glue
in a superior terror; be thy taut
flesh silver, like the currency of faint
cities eternal—ere the sinless taint
of thy long sinful arms about me dream
shall my love wholly taste thee as a new
wine from steep hills by darkness softly brought—

(be with me in the sacred witchery
of almostness which May makes follow soon
on the sweet heels of passed afterday,
clothe thy soul's coming merely, with a croon
of mingling robes musically revealed
in rareness: let thy twain eyes deeply wield
a noise of petals falling silently
through the far-spaced possible nearaway
from huge trees drenched by a rounding moon)

I I

Always before your voice my soul
half-beautiful and wholly droll
is as some smooth and awkward foal,
whereof young moons begin
the newness of his skin,

so of my stupid sincere youth
the exquisite failure uncouth
discovers a trembling and smooth
Unstrength, against the strong
silences of your song·

or as a single lamb whose sheen
of full unsheared fleece is mean
beside its lovelier friends, between
your thoughts more white than wool
My thought is sorrowful:

but my heart smote in trembling thirds
of anguish quivers to your words,
As to a flight of thirty birds
shakes with a thickening fright
the sudden fooled light.

it is the autumn of a year:
When through the thin air stooped with fear,
across the harvest whitely peer
empty of surprise
death's faultless eyes

(whose hand my folded soul shall know
while on faint hills do frailly go
The peaceful terrors of the snow,
and before your dead face
which sleeps, a dream shall pass)

and these my days their sounds and flowers
Fall in a pride of petaled hours,
like flowers at the feet of mowers
whose bodies strong with love
through meadows hugely move.

yet what am i that such and such
mysteries very simply touch
me, whose heart-wholeness overmuch
Expects of your hair pale,
a terror musical?

while in an earthless hour my fond
soul seriously yearns beyond
this fern of sunset frond on frond
opening in a rare
Slowness of gloried air . . .

The flute of morning stilled in noon—
noon the implacable bassoon—
now Twilight seeks the thrill of moon,
washed with a wild and thin
despair of violin

III

Thy fingers make early flowers of
all things.
thy hair mostly the hours love:
a smoothness which
sings, saying
(though love be a day)
do not fear, we will go amaying.

thy whitest feet crisply are straying.
Always
thy moist eyes are at kisses playing,
whose strangeness much
says; singing
(though love be a day)
for which girl art thou flowers bringing?

To be thy lips is a sweet thing
and small.
Death, Thee i call rich beyond wishing
if this thou catch,
else missing.
(though love be a day
and life be nothing, it shall not stop kissing).

IV

All in green went my love riding
on a great horse of gold
into the silver dawn.

four lean hounds crouched low and smiling
the merry deer ran before.

Fleeter be they than dappled dreams
the swift sweet deer
the red rare deer.

Four red roebuck at a white water
the cruel bugle sang before.

Horn at hip went my love riding
riding the echo down
into the silver dawn.

four lean hounds crouched low and smiling
the level meadows ran before.

Softer be they than slippered sleep
the lean lithe deer
the fleet flown deer.

Four fleet does at a gold valley
the famished arrow sang before.

Bow at belt went my love riding
riding the mountain down
into the silver dawn.

four lean hounds crouched low and smiling
the sheer peaks ran before.

Paler be they than daunting death
the sleek slim deer
the tall tense deer.

Four tall stags at a green mountain
the lucky hunter sang before.

All in green went my love riding
on a great horse of gold
into the silver dawn.

four lean hounds crouched low and smiling
my heart fell dead before.

V

Doll's boy 's asleep
under a stile
he sees eight and twenty
ladies in a line

the first lady
says to nine ladies
his lips drink water
but his heart drinks wine

the tenth lady
says to nine ladies
they must chain his foot
for his wrist 's too fine

the nineteenth
says to nine ladies
you take his mouth
for his eyes are mine.

Doll's boy 's asleep
under the stile
for every mile the feet go
the heart goes nine

VI

when god lets my body be

From each brave eye shall sprout a tree
fruit that dangles therefrom

the purpled world will dance upon
Between my lips which did sing

a rose shall beget the spring
that maidens whom passion wastes

will lay between their little breasts
My strong fingers beneath the snow

Into strenuous birds shall go
my love walking in the grass

their wings will touch with her face
and all the while shall my heart be

With the bulge and nuzzle of the sea

PUELLA MEA

Harun Omar and Master Hafiz
keep your dead beautiful ladies.
Mine is a little lovelier
than any of your ladies were.

In her perfectest array
my lady, moving in the day,
is a little stranger thing
than crisp Sheba with her king
in the morning wandering.
  Through the young and awkward hours
my lady perfectly moving,
through the new world scarce astir
my fragile lady wandering
in whose perishable poise
is the mystery of Spring
(with her beauty more than snow
dexterous and fugitive
my very frail lady drifting
distinctly, moving like a myth
in the uncertain morning, with
April feet like sudden flowers
and all her body filled with May)
—moving in the unskilful day
my lady utterly alive,
to me is a more curious thing
(a thing more nimble and complete)
than ever to Judea's king
were the shapely sharp cunning
and withal delirious feet
of the Princess Salomé
carefully dancing in the noise
of Herod's silence, long ago.

If she a little turn her head
i know that i am wholly dead:
nor ever did on such a throat
the lips of Tristram slowly dote,
La beale Isoud whose leman was.
And if my lady look at me
(with her eyes which like two elves
incredibly amuse themselves)
with a look of færie,
perhaps a little suddenly
(as sometimes the improbable
beauty of my lady will)
—at her glance my spirit shies
rearing (as in the miracle
of a lady who had eyes
which the king's horses might not kill.)
  But should my lady smile, it were
a flower of so pure surprise
(it were so very new a flower,
a flower so frail, a flower so glad)
as trembling used to yield with dew
when the world was young and new
(a flower such as the world had
in Springtime when the world was mad
and Launcelot spoke to Guenever,
a flower which most heavy hung
with silence when the world was young
and Diarmid looked in Grania's eyes.)
  But should my lady's beauty play
at not speaking (sometimes as
it will) the silence of her face
doth immediately make
in my heart so great a noise,
as in the sharp and thirsty blood
of Paris would not all the Troys
of Helen's beauty: never did
Lord Jason (in impossible things
victorious impossibly)
so wholly burn, to undertake
Medea's rescuing eyes; nor he
when swooned the white egyptian day
who with Egypt's body lay.

Lovely as those ladies were
mine is a little lovelier.

And if she speak in her frail way,
it is wholly to bewitch
my smallest thought with a most swift
radiance wherein slowly drift
murmurous things divinely bright;
it is foolingly to smite
my spirit with the lithe free twitch
of scintillant space, with the cool writhe
of gloom truly which syncopate
some sunbeam's skilful fingerings;
it is utterly to lull
with foliate inscrutable
sweetness my soul obedient;
it is to stroke my being with
numbing forests frolicsome,
fleetly mystical, aroam
with keen creatures of idiom
(beings alert and innocent
very deftly upon which
indolent miracles impinge)
—it is distinctly to confute
my reason with the deep caress
of every most shy thing and mute,
it is to quell me with the twinge
of all living intense things.
    Never my soul so fortunate
is (past the luck of all dead men
and loving) as invisibly when
upon her palpable solitude
a furtive occult fragrance steals,
a gesture of immaculate
perfume—whereby (with fear aglow)
my soul is wont wholly to know
the poignant instantaneous fern
whose scrupulous enchanted fronds
toward all things intrinsic yearn,
the immanent subliminal
fern of her delicious voice

(of her voice which always dwells
beside the vivid magical
impetuous and utter ponds
of dream; and very secret food
its leaves inimitable find
beyond the white authentic springs,
beyond the sweet instinctive wells,
which make to flourish the minute
spontaneous meadow of her mind)
—the vocal fern, always which feels
the keen ecstatic actual tread
(and thereto perfectly responds)
of all things exquisite and dead,
all living things and beautiful.

(Caliph and king their ladies had
to love them and to make them glad,
when the world was young and mad,
in the city of Bagdad—
mine is a little lovelier
than any of those ladies were.)

Her body is most beauteous,
being for all things amorous
fashioned very curiously
of roses and of ivory.
The immaculate crisp head
is such as only certain dead
and careful painters love to use
for their youngest angels (whose
praising bodies in a row
between slow glories fleetly go.)
Upon a keen and lovely throat
the strangeness of her face doth float,
which in eyes and lips consists
—always upon the mouth there trysts
curvingly a fragile smile
which like a flower lieth (while
within the eyes is dimly heard
a wistful and precarious bird.)
Springing from fragrant shoulders small,
ardent, and perfectly withal

smooth to stroke and sweet to see
as a supple and young tree,
her slim lascivious arms alight
in skilful wrists which hint at flight
—my lady's very singular
and slenderest hands moreover are
(which as lilies smile and quail)
of all things perfect the most frail.

(Whoso rideth in the tale
of Chaucer knoweth many a pair
of companions blithe and fair;
who to walk with Master Gower
in Confessio doth prefer
shall not lack for beauty there,
nor he that will amaying go
with my lord Boccaccio—
whoso knocketh at the door
of Marie and of Maleore
findeth of ladies goodly store
whose beauty did in nothing err.
If to me there shall appear
than a rose more sweetly known,
more silently than a flower,
my lady naked in her hair—
i for those ladies nothing care
nor any lady dead and gone.)

Each tapering breast is firm and smooth
that in a lovely fashion doth
from my lady's body grow;
as morning may a lily know,
her petaled flesh doth entertain
the adroit blood's mysterious skein
(but like some passionate earlier
flower, the snow will oft utter,
whereof the year has perfect bliss—
for each breast a blossom is,
which being a little while caressed
its fragrance makes the lover blest.)
Her waist is a most tiny hinge
of flesh, a winsome thing and strange;

apt in my hand warmly to lie
it is a throbbing neck whereby
to grasp the belly's ample vase
(that urgent urn which doth amass
for whoso drinks, a dizzier wine
than should the grapes of heaven combine
with earth's madness)—'tis a gate
unto a palace intricate
(whereof the luscious pillars rise
which are her large and shapely thighs)
in whose dome the trembling bliss
of a kingdom wholly is.
   Beneath her thighs such legs are seen
as were the pride of the world's queen:
each is a verb, miraculous
inflected oral devious,
beneath the body's breathing noun
(moreover the delicious frown
of the grave great sensual knees
well might any monarch please.)
Each ankle is divinely shy;
as if for fear you would espy
the little distinct foot (if whose
very minuteness doth abuse
reason, why then the artificer
did most exquisitely err.)

When the world was like a song
heard behind a golden door,
poet and sage and caliph had
to love them and to make them glad
ladies with lithe eyes and long
(when the world was like a flower
Omar Hafiz and Harun
loved their ladies in the moon)
—fashioned very curiously
of roses and of ivory
if naked she appear to me
my flesh is an enchanted tree;
with her lips' most frail parting
my body hears the cry of Spring,
and with their frailest syllable
its leaves go crisp with miracle.

Love!—maker of my lady,
in that always beyond this
poem or any poem she
of whose body words are afraid
perfectly beautiful is,
forgive these words which i have made.
And never boast your dead beauties,
you greatest lovers in the world!
who with Grania strangely fled,
who with Egypt went to bed,
whom white-thighed Semiramis
put up her mouth to wholly kiss—
never boast your dead beauties,
mine being unto me sweeter
(of whose shy delicious glance
things which never more shall be,
perfect things of færie,
are intense inhabitants;
in whose warm superlative
body do distinctly live
all sweet cities passed away—
in her flesh at break of day
are the smells of Nineveh,
in her eyes when day is gone
are the cries of Babylon.)
Diarmid Paris and Solomon,
Omar Harun and Master Hafiz,
to me your ladies are all one—
keep your dead beautiful ladies.

Eater of all things lovely—Time!
upon whose watering lips the world
poises a moment (futile, proud,
a costly morsel of sweet tears)
gesticulates, and disappears—
of all dainties which do crowd
gaily upon oblivion
sweeter than any there is one;
to touch it is the fear of rhyme—
in life's very fragile hour
(when the world was like a tale

made of laughter and of dew,
was a flight, a flower, a flame,
was a tendril fleetly curled
upon frailness) used to stroll
(very slowly) one or two
ladies like flowers made,
softly used to wholly move
slender ladies made of dream
(in the lazy world and new
sweetly used to laugh and love
ladies with crisp eyes and frail,
in the city of Bagdad.)

Keep your dead beautiful ladies
Harun Omar and Master Hafiz.

CHANSONS INNOCENTES

I

in Just-
spring   when the world is mud-
luscious the little
lame balloonman

whistles   far   and wee

and eddieandbill come
running from marbles and
piracies and it's
spring

when the world is puddle-wonderful

the queer
old balloonman whistles
far   and   wee
and bettyandisbel come dancing

from hop-scotch and jump-rope and

it's
spring
and
   the

      goat-footed

balloonMan   whistles
far
and
wee

I I

hist   whist
little ghostthings
tip-toe
twinkle-toe

little twitchy
witches and tingling
goblins
hob-a-nob   hob-a-**nob**

little hoppy happy
toad in tweeds
tweeds
little itchy mousies

with scuttling
eyes   rustle and **run**   **and**
hidehidehide
whisk

whisk   look out for the old **woman**
with the wart on her nose
what she'll do to yer
nobody knows

for she knows the devil   **ooch**
the devil   ouch
the devil
ach   the great

green
dancing
devil
devil

devil
devil

wheeEEE

III

Tumbling-hair
            picker of buttercups
                        violets
dandelions
And the big bullying daisies
                        through the field wonderful
with eyes a little sorry
Another comes
            also picking flowers

ORIENTALE

I

i spoke to thee
with a smile and thou didst not
answer
thy mouth is as
a chord of crimson music
                        Come hither
O thou, is life not a smile?

i spoke to thee with
a song and thou
didst not listen
thine eyes are as a vase
of divine silence
                        Come hither
O thou, is life not a song?

i spoke
to thee with a soul and
thou didst not wonder
thy face is as a dream locked
in white fragrance
                    Come hither
O thou, is life not love?

i speak to
thee with a sword
and thou art silent
thy breast is as a tomb
softer than flowers
                    Come hither
O thou, is love not death?

I I

lean candles hunger in
the silence a
brown god
smiles between greentwittering

smokes   from broken eyes
a sound
of strangling breasts and bestial
grovelling

hands rasps the purple
dark-
ness
a

worshipper
prostrate within twitching shadow
lolls

sobbing

with lust

III

my love
thy hair is one kingdom
  the king whereof is darkness
thy forehead is a flight of flowers

thy head is a quick forest
  filled with sleeping birds
thy breasts are swarms of white bees
  upon the bough of thy body
thy body to me is April
in whose armpits is the approach of spring

thy thighs are white horses yoked to a chariot
  of kings
they are the striking of a good minstrel
between them is always a pleasant song

my love
thy head is a casket
  of the cool jewel of thy mind
the hair of thy head is one warrior
  innocent of defeat
thy hair upon thy shoulders is an army
  with victory and with trumpets

thy legs are the trees of dreaming
whose fruit is the very eatage of forgetfulness

thy lips are satraps in scarlet
  in whose kiss is the combining of kings
thy wrists
are holy
  which are the keepers of the keys of thy blood
thy feet upon thy ankles are flowers in vases
  of silver

in thy beauty is the dilemma of flutes

  thy eyes are the betrayal
of bells comprehended through incense

I V

listen
beloved
i dreamed
 it appeared that you thought to
 escape me and became a great
 lily atilt on
 insolent
 waters but i was aware of
 fragrance and i came riding upon
 a horse of porphyry into the
 waters i rode down the red
 horse shrieking from splintering
 foam caught you clutched you upon my
 mouth
listen
beloved
 i dreamed in my dream you had
 desire to thwart me and became
 a little bird and hid
 in a tree of tall marble
 from a great way i distinguished
 singing and i came
 riding upon a scarlet sunset
 trampling the night easily
 from the shocked impossible
 tower i caught
 you strained you
 broke you upon my blood
listen
 beloved i dreamed
 i thought you would have deceived
 me and became a star in the kingdom
 of heaven
 through day and space i saw you close
 your eyes and i came riding
 upon a thousand crimson years arched with agony
 i reined them in tottering before
 the throne and as
 they shied at the automaton moon from
 the transplendent hand of sombre god
 i picked you
as an apple is picked by the little peasants for their girls

V

unto thee i
burn incense
the bowl crackles
upon the gloom arise purple pencils

fluent spires of fragrance
the bowl
seethes
a flutter of stars

a turbulence of forms
delightful with indefinable flowering,
the air is
deep with desirable flowers

i think
thou lovest incense
for in the ambiguous faint aspirings
the indolent frail ascensions,

of thy smile rises the immaculate
sorrow
of thy low
hair flutter the level litanies

unto thee i burn
incense, over the dim smoke
straining my lips are vague with
ecstasy my palpitating breasts inhale the

slow
supple
flower
of thy beauty, my heart discovers thee

unto
whom i
burn
olbanum

VI

1.

the emperor
sleeps in a palace of porphyry
which was a million years building
he takes the air in a howdah
of jasper beneath saffron
umbrellas
upon an elephant
twelve feet high
behind whose ear
sits always a crowned
king twir-
ling an
ankus of
ebony
the fountains of the emperor's
palace run sunlight and
moonlight and the emperor's
elephant is a thousand years old

the harem of
the emperor
is carpeted with
gold cloth
from the
ceiling (one
diamond timid
with nesting incense)
fifty
marble
pillars
slipped from immeasurable
height, fall, fifty, silent

in the incense is tangled a cool moon

there are thrice-three-hundred
doors carven of chalcedony and
before every door a naked
eunuch watches
on their heads turbans of a hundred
colours
in their hands scimitars like windy torches
each
is
blacker than oblivion

the ladies
of the emperor's
harem are queens
of all the earth and the rings
upon their hands are from mines
a mile deep
but the body of
the queen of queens is
more transparent
than water, she is softer than birds

2.

when the emperor is very
amorous he reclines upon
the couch of couches and
beckons   with
the little
finger of his left
hand
      then the
thrice-three-hundredth
door is opened by the tallest
eunuch and the queen
of queens comes
forth
ankles
musical with large pearls
kingdoms in her ears

at the feet of
the emperor a cithern-
player squats with
quiveringgold
body
behind
the emperor ten
elected warriors with
bodies of lazy jade
and twitching
eyelids
finger
their
unquiet
spears

the queen of queens is dancing

her subtle
body weaving
insinuating upon the gold cloth
incessantly creates patterns of sudden
lust
her
stealing body ex-
pending gathering pouring upon itself   stiffenS
to a
white thorn
of desire

the taut neck of the citharede wags
in the dust the ghastly warriors
amber with lust breathe
together   the emperor, exerting
himself among his pillows throws
jewels at the queen of queens and
white money upon her nakedness
he
nods
       and all
depart through the bruised air aflutter with pearls

3.

they are
alone
he beckons, she rises she
stands
a moment
in the passion of the fifty
pillars
listening

while the queens of all the
earth writhe upon deep rugs

AMORES

I

consider O
woman this
my body.
for it has

lain
with empty arms
upon the giddy hills
to dream of you,

approve these
firm unsated
eyes
which have beheld

night's speechless carnival
the painting
of the dark
with meteors

streaming from playful
immortal hands
the bursting
of the wafted stars

(in time to come you shall
remember of this night amazing
ecstasies   slowly,
in the glutted

heart fleet
flowerterrible
memories
shall

rise, slowly
return upon the
                    red elected lips

scaleless visions)

II

there is a
moon sole
in the blue
night

        amorous of waters
tremulous,
blinded with silence the
undulous heaven yearns where

in tense starlessness
anoint with ardor
the yellow lover

stands in the dumb dark
svelte
and
urgent

        (again
love i slowly
gather
of thy languorous mouth the

thrilling
flower)

as is the sea
from god's
hands which se...
to sleep upon the...

and the earth withe...
the moon crumbles
one by one
stars flutter into dust

but the sea
does not change
and she goes forth out of ha...
she returns into hands

and is with sleep . . . .

love,
    the breaking

of your
       soul
       upon
my lips

IV

if i believe
in death be sure
of this
it is

because you have loved me,
moon and sunset
stars and flowers
gold crescendo and silver muting

of seatides
i trusted not,
        one night
when in my fingers

drooped your shining body
when my heart
sang between your perfect
breasts

darkness and beauty of stars
was on my mouth petals danced
against my eyes
and down

the singing reaches of
my soul
spoke
the green-

greeting pale-
departing irrevocable
sea
i knew thee death.

          and when
i have offered up each fragrant
night, when all my days
shall have before a certain

face become
white
perfume
only,

    from the ashes
then
thou wilt rise and thou
wilt come to her and brush

the mischief from her eyes and fold
her
mouth the new
flower with

thy unimaginable
wings, where dwells the breath
of all persisting stars

V

the glory is fallen out of
the sky the last immortal
leaf
is

dead and the gold
year
a formal spasm
in the

dust
this is the passing of all shining things
therefore we also
blandly

into receptive
earth, O let
us
descend

take
shimmering wind
these fragile splendors from
us crumple them hide

them in thy breath drive
them in nothingness
for we
would sleep

this is the passing of all shining things
no lingering no backward-
wondering be unto
us O

soul, but straight
glad feet fearruining
and glorygirded
faces

lead us
into the
serious
steep

darkness

VI

i like
to think that on
the flower you gave me when we
loved

      the far-
departed mouth sweetly-saluted
lingers.
           if one marvel

seeing the hunger of my
lips for a dead thing,
i shall instruct
him silently with becoming

steps to seek
your face   and i
entreat, by certain foolish perfect
hours

       dead too,
if that he come receive
him as your lover sumptuously
being

kind
      because i trust him to
your grace, and for
in his own land

he is called death.

VII

O Distinct
Lady of my unkempt adoration
if i have made
a fragile certain

song under the window of your soul
it is not like any songs
(the singers the others
they have been faithful

to many things and which
die
i have been sometimes true
to Nothing and which lives

they were fond of the handsome
moon   never spoke ill of the
pretty stars   and to
the serene the complicated

and the obvious
they were faithful
and which i despise,
frankly

admitting i have been true
only to the noise of worms.
in the eligible day
under the unaccountable sun)

Distinct Lady
swiftly take
my fragile certain song
that we may watch together

how behind the doomed
exact smile of life's
placid obscure palpable
carnival where to a normal

melody of probable violins dance
the square virtues and the oblong sins
perfectly
gesticulate the accurate

strenuous lips of incorruptible
Nothing   under the ample
sun, under the insufficient
day under the noise of worms

VIII

your little voice
              Over the wires came leaping
and i felt suddenly
dizzy
       With the jostling and shouting of merry flowers
wee skipping high-heeled flames
courtesied before my eyes
                           or twinkling over to my side
Looked up
with impertinently exquisite faces
floating hands were laid upon me
I was whirled and tossed into delicious dancing
up
Up
with the pale important
                    stars and the Humorous
                                        moon
dear girl
How i was crazy how i cried when i heard
                                  over time
and tide and death
leaping
Sweetly
       your voice

LA GUERRE

I

the bigness of cannon
is skilful,

but i have seen
death's clever enormous voice
which hides in a fragility
of poppies . . . .

i say that sometimes
on these long talkative animals
are laid fists of huger silence.

I have seen all the silence
filled with vivid noiseless boys

at Roupy
i have seen
between barrages,

the night utter ripe unspeaking girls.

II

O sweet spontaneous
earth how often have
the
doting

        fingers of
prurient philosophers pinched
and
poked

thee
, has the naughty thumb
of science prodded
thy

beauty   . how
often have religions taken
thee upon their scraggy knees
squeezing and

buffeting thee that thou mightest conceive
gods
    (but
true

to the incomparable
couch of death thy
rhythmic
lover

    thou answerest

them only with

    spring)

IMPRESSIONS

I

the sky a silver
dissonance by the correct
fingers of April
resolved

    into a
clutter of trite jewels

now like a moth with stumbling

wings flutters and flops along the
grass collides with trees and
houses and finally,
butts into the river

II

writhe and
gape of tortured

 perspective
rasp and graze of splintered

normality
           crackle and
           sag
of planes   clamors of
collision
collapse   As

peacefully,
lifted
into the awful beauty
                              of sunset

                              the young city
putting off dimension with a blush
enters
the becoming garden of her agony

III

i was considering how
within night's loose
sack a star's
nibbling in-

fin
-i-
tes-
i
-mal-
ly devours

darkness the
hungry star
which
will e

-ven
tu-
al
-ly jiggle
the bait of
dawn and be jerked

into

eternity.   when over my head **a**
shooting
star
Bur   s

       (t
            into a stale **shriek**
like an alarm-clock)

I V

the hours rise up putting off stars and it is
dawn
into the street of the sky light walks scattering poems

on earth a candle is
extinguished   the city
wakes
with a song upon her
mouth having death in her eyes

and it is dawn
the world
goes forth to murder dreams . . . .

i see in the street where strong
men are digging bread
and i see the brutal faces of
people contented hideous hopeless cruel **happy**

and it is day,

in the mirror
i see a frail
man
dreaming
dreams
dreams in the mirror

and it
is dusk   on earth

a candle is lighted
and it is dark.
the people are in their houses
the frail man is in his bed
the city

sleeps with death upon her mouth having a song in her eyes
the hours descend,
putting on stars . . . .

in the street of the sky night walks scattering poems

                         V

            stinging
            gold swarms
            upon the spires
            silver

                   chants the litanies the
            great bells are ringing with rose
            the lewd fat bells
                         and a tall

            wind
            is dragging
            the
            sea

            with

            dream

            -S

PORTRAITS

I

the
nimble
heat
had

long on a certain
taut precarious
holiday
frighteningly

performed
and
at tremont and bromfield i
paused a moment because

on the frying
curb the
quiet face
lay

which had been dorothy
and once
permitted
me for

twenty
iron
men
her common purple

soul
the absurd eyelids sulked
enormous
sobs puckered the foolish

breasts the
droll
mouth
wilted

and not old, harry, a
woman in the crowd
whinnied and a man squeezing her
waist said

the cop's rung for the
wagon but as i was
lifting the horror
of her toylike

head and vainly
tried to
catch one funny
hand opening the hard great

eyes to noone in particular she
gasped almost
loudly
i'm

so
drunG

k, dear

I I

of evident invisibles
exquisite the hovering

at the dark portals

of hurt girl eyes

sincere with wonder

a poise a wounding
a beautiful suppression

the accurate boy mouth

now droops the faun head

now the intimate flower dreams

of parted lips
dim upon the syrinx

III

between nose-red gross
walls   sprawling with tipsy
tables the abominable
floor belches smoky

laughter into the filigree
frame of a microscopic
stage whose jouncing curtain.   , rises
upon one startling doll

undressed in unripe green with
nauseous spiderlegs
and excremental
hair and the eyes of the mother of

god who spits seeds of dead
song about home and love from her
transfigured face a queer
pulp of ecstasy

while in the battered
bodies the odd unlovely
souls struggle   slowly   and   writhe
like caught.brave:flies;

I V

i walked the boulevard

i saw a dirty child
skating on noisy wheels of joy

pathetic dress fluttering

behind her a mothermonster
with red grumbling face

cluttered in pursuit

pleasantly elephantine

while nearby the father

a thick cheerful man

with majestic bulbous lips
and forlorn piggish hands

joked to a girlish whore

with busy rhythmic mouth
and silly purple eyelids

of how she was with child

V

the young
man sitting
in Dick Mid's Place
said to Death

teach me of her
Thy yonder servant who
in Thy very house silently
sits looking beyond the

kissing and the striving of
that old man who at her
redstone mouth renews his
childhood

and He
said
"willingly
for the tale is short

it was
i think yourself delivered into
both my hands herself to
always keep"

always?
the young
man sitting in Dick Mid's
Place

asked
"always"
Death
said

"then as i recollect her
girlhood was by the kindly
lips and body fatherly of a
romantic tired business man

somewhat tweaked and dinted
then
did my servant
become of the company of those

ladies with faces painteaten
and bodies lightly
desperate certainly wherefrom
departed is youth's indispensable

illusion"

VI

but the other
day i was passing a certain
gate,   rain
fell (as it will

in spring)
ropes
of silver gliding from sunny
thunder into freshness

as if god's flowers were
pulling upon bells of
gold   i looked
up

and
thought to myself   Death
and will You with
elaborate fingers possibly touch

the pink hollyhock existence whose
pansy eyes look from morning till
night into the street
unchangingly   the always

old lady always sitting in her
gentle window like
a reminiscence
partaken

softly   at whose gate smile
always the chosen
flowers of reminding

VII

the rose
is dying the
lips of an old man murder

the petals
hush
mysteriously
invisible mourners move
with prose faces and sobbing, garments
The symbol of the rose

motionless
with grieving feet and
wings
mounts

against the margins of steep song
a stallion sweetness   , the

lips of an old man murder

the petals.

VIII

Buffalo Bill 's
defunct
          who used to
          ride a watersmooth-silver
                              stallion
and break onetwothreefourfive pigeonsjustlikethat
                                        Jesus

he was a handsome man
                    and what i want to know is
how do you like your blueeyed boy
Mister Death

IX

spring omnipotent goddess thou dost
inveigle into crossing sidewalks the
unwary june-bug and the frivolous angleworm
thou dost persuade to serenade his
lady the musical tom-cat, thou stuffest
the parks with overgrown pimply
cavaliers and gumchewing giggly
girls and not content
Spring, with this
thou hangest canary-birds in parlor windows

spring slattern of seasons you
have dirty legs and a muddy
petticoat, drowsy is your
mouth your eyes are sticky
with dreams and you have
a sloppy body
from being brought to bed of crocuses
When you sing in your whiskey-voice

                                        the grass
rises on the head of the earth
and all the trees are put on edge

spring,
of the jostle of
thy breasts and the slobber
of your thighs
i am so very
                glad that the soul inside me Hollers
for thou comest and your hands
are the snow
and thy fingers are the rain,
and i hear
the screech of dissonant
flowers, and most of all

i hear your stepping
                        freakish feet
                        feet incorrigible
    ragging the world,

X

somebody knew Lincoln somebody Xerxes

this man: a narrow thudding timeshaped face
plus innocuous winking hands, carefully
inhabits number 1 on something street

Spring comes
                    the lean and definite houses

are troubled. A sharp blue day
fills with peacefully leaping air
the minute mind of the world.
The lean and

definite houses are
troubled. in the sunset their chimneys converse
angrily, their
roofs are nervous with the soft furious
light, and while fire-escapes and
roofs and chimneys and while roofs and fire-escapes and
chimneys and while chimneys and fire-escapes
and roofs are talking rapidly all together there happens
Something, and They

cease(and
one by one are turned suddenly and softly
into irresponsible toys.)
                            when this man with

the brittle legs winces
swiftly out of number 1 someThing
street and trickles carefully into the park
sits

Down.   pigeons circle
around and around and around the

irresponsible toys
circle wildly in the slow-ly-in creasing fragility
—. Dogs
bark
children
play
-ing
      Are

in the beautiful nonsense of twilight

and somebody Napoleon

POST IMPRESSIONS

I

beyond the brittle towns asleep
i look where stealing needles of foam
in the last light

thread the creeping shores

as out of dumb strong hands infinite

the erect deep upon me
in the last light
pours its eyeless miles

the chattering sunset ludicrously
dies, i hear only tidewings

in the last light
twitching at the world

II

the moon is hiding in
her hair.
The
lily
of heaven
full of all dreams,
draws down.

cover her briefness in singing
close her with intricate faint birds
by daisies and twilights
Deepen her,

Recite
upon her
flesh
the rain's

pearls singly-whispering.

III

into the strenuous briefness
Life:
handorgans and April
darkness, friends

i charge laughing.
Into the hair-thin tints
of yellow dawn,
into the women-coloured twilight

i smilingly
glide. I
into the big vermillion departure
swim, sayingly;

(Do you think?) the
i do, world
is probably made
of roses & hello:

(of solongs and, ashes)

IV

i am going to utter a tree, Nobody
shall stop me

but first
earth   , the reckless oral darkness
raging with thin impulse

i will have

a

   dream
   i
   think it shall be roses and
spring will bring her
worms rushing through loam.

(afterward i'll
climb
by tall careful muscles

into nervous and accurate silence . . . . But   first

you)

press easily
at first, it will be leaves
and a little harder
for roses
only a little harder

last   we
on the groaning flame of neat huge
trudging kiss moistly climbing hideously with
large
minute
hips, O

          .press

worms rushing slowly through loam

V

any man is wonderful
and a formula
a bit of tobacco and gladness
plus little derricks of gesture

any skyscraper
bulges in the looseness of morning
but in twilight becomes
unutterably crisp

a thing,
which tightens
caught
in the hoisting light

any woman is smooth and ridiculous
a polite uproar of knuckling silent planes
a nudging bulb silkenly brutal
a devout flexion

VI

at the head of this street a gasping organ is waving motheaten tunes. a fatish hand turns the crank; the box sprouts
fairies, out of it sour gnomes tumble clumsily, the little box
is spilling rancid elves upon neat sunlight into the flowerstricken air which is filthy with agile swarming sonal creatures

—Children, stand with circular frightened faces glaring at
the shabby tiny smiling, man in whose hand the crank goes
desperately, round and round pointing to the queer monkey

(if you toss him a coin he will pick it cleverly from, the air
and stuff it seriously in, his minute pocket) Sometimes he
does not catch a piece of money and then his master will
yell at him over the music and jerk the little string and the
monkey will sit, up, and look at, you with his solemn blinky
eyeswhichneversmile and after he has caught a, penny or
three, pennies he will be thrown a peanut (which he will

open skilfully with his, mouth carefully holding, it, in his little toylike hand) and then he will stiff-ly throw the shell away with a small bored gesture that makes the children laugh.

But i don't, the crank goes round desperate elves and hopeless gnomes and frantic fairies gush clumsily from the battered box fatish and mysterious the flowerstricken sunlight is thickening dizzily is reeling gently the street and the children and the monkeyandtheorgan and the man are dancing slowly are tottering up and down in a trembly mist of atrocious melody . . . . tiniest dead tunes crawl upon my face my hair is lousy with mutilated singing microscopic things in my ears scramble faintly tickling putrescent atomies,

       and

               i feel the jerk of the little string! the tiny smiling shabby man is yelling over the music i understand him i shove my round red hat back on my head i sit up and blink at you with my solemn eyeswhichneversmile

yes, By god.
for i am they are pointing at the queer monkey with a little oldish doll-like face and hairy arms like an ogre and rubbercoloured hands and feet filled with quick fingers and a remarkable tail which is allbyitself alive. (and he has a little red coat with i have a real pocket in it and the round funny hat with a big feather is tied under myhis chin.) that climbs and cries and runs and floats like a toy on the end of a string

Chimneys

SONNETS—REALITIES

I

the Cambridge ladies who live in furnished souls
are unbeautiful and have comfortable minds
(also, with the church's protestant blessings
daughters, unscented shapeless spirited)
they believe in Christ and Longfellow, both dead,
are invariably interested in so many things—
at the present writing one still finds
delighted fingers knitting for the is it Poles?
perhaps. While permanent faces coyly bandy
scandal of Mrs. N and Professor D
. . . . the Cambridge ladies do not care, above
Cambridge if sometimes in its box of
sky lavender and cornerless, the
moon rattles like a fragment of angry candy

II

goodby Betty, don't remember me
pencil your eyes dear and have a good time
with the tall tight boys at Tabari'
s, keep your teeth snowy, stick to beer and lime,
wear dark, and where your meeting breasts are round
have roses darling, it's all i ask of you—
but that when light fails and this sweet profound
Paris moves with lovers, two and two
bound for themselves, when passionately dusk
brings softly down the perfume of the world
(and just as smaller stars begin to husk
heaven) you, you exactly paled and curled

with mystic lips take twilight where i know:
proving to Death that Love is so and so.

III

ladies and gentlemen this little girl
with the good teeth and small important breasts
(is it the Frolic or the Century whirl?
one's memory indignantly protests)
this little dancer with the tightened eyes
crisp ogling shoulders and the ripe quite too
large lips always clenched faintly, wishes you
with all her fragile might to not surmise
she dreamed one afternoon

　　　　　　　. . . . or maybe read?

of a time when the beautiful most of her
(this here and This, do you get me?)
will maybe dance and maybe sing and be
absitively posolutely dead,
like Coney Island in winter

IV

when you rang at Dick Mid's Place
the madam was a bulb stuck in the door.
a fang of wincing gas showed how
hair, in two fists of shrill colour,
clutched the dull volume of her tumbling face
scribbled with a big grin. her sow-
eyes clicking mischief from thick lids.
the chunklike nose on which always the four
tablets of perspiration erectly sitting.
—If they knew you at Dick Mid's
the three trickling chins began to traipse
into the cheeks "eet smeestaire steevensun
kum een, dare ease Bet, an Leelee, an dee beeg wun"
her handless wrists did gooey severe shapes.

V

"kitty". sixteen, 5′ 1″, white, prostitute.

ducking always the touch of must and shall,
whose slippery body is Death's littlest pal,

skilled in quick softness. Unspontaneous. cute.

the signal perfume of whose unrepute
focusses in the sweet slow animal
bottomless eyes importantly banal,

Kitty. a whore. Sixteen
                              you corking brute
amused from time to time by clever drolls
fearsomely who do keep their sunday flower.
The babybreasted broad "kitty" twice eight

—beer nothing, the lady'll have a whiskey-sour—

whose least amazing smile is the most great
common divisor of unequal souls.

V I

when thou hast taken thy last applause, and when
the final curtain strikes the world away,
leaving to shadowy silence and dismay
that stage which shall not know thy smile again,
lingering a little while i see thee then
ponder the tinsel part they let thee play;
i see the large lips vivid, the face grey,
and silent smileless eyes of Magdalen.
The lights have laughed their last; without, the street
darkling awaiteth her whose feet have trod
the silly souls of men to golden dust:
she pauses on the lintel of defeat,
her heart breaks in a smile—and she is Lust . . . .

mine also, little painted poem of god

SONNETS—UNREALITIES

I

it may not always be so; and i say
that if your lips, which i have loved, should touch
another's, and your dear strong fingers clutch
his heart, as mine in time not far away;
if on another's face your sweet hair lay
in such a silence as i know, or such
great writhing words as, uttering overmuch,
stand helplessly before the spirit at bay;

if this should be, i say if this should be—
you of my heart, send me a little word;
that i may go unto him, and take his hands,
saying, Accept all happiness from me.
Then shall i turn my face, and hear one bird
sing terribly afar in the lost lands.

II

god gloats upon Her stunning flesh. Upon
the reachings of Her green body among
unseen things, things obscene (Whose fingers young

the caving ages curiously con)

—but the lunge of Her hunger softly flung
over the gasping shores
                        leaves his smile wan,
and his blood stopped hears in the frail anon

the shovings and the lovings of Her tongue.

god Is The Sea. All terrors of his being
quake before this its hideous Work most old
Whose battening gesture prophecies a freeing

of ghostly chaos
            in this dangerous night
through moaned space god worships God—

                         (behold!
where chaste stars writhe captured in brightening fright)

III

it is at moments after i have dreamed
of the rare entertainment of your eyes,
when(being fool to fancy)i have deemed

with your peculiar mouth my heart made wise;
at moments when the glassy darkness holds

the genuine apparition of your smile
(it was through tears always)and silence moulds
such strangeness as was mine a little while;

moments when my once more illustrious arms
are filled with fascination, when my breast
wears the intolerant brightness of your charms:

one pierced moment whiter than the rest

—turning from the tremendous lie of sleep
i watch the roses of the day grow deep.

IV

when citied day with the sonorous homes
of light swiftly sink in the sorrowful hour,
thy counted petals O tremendous flower
on whose huge heart prospecting darkness roams

torture my spirit with the exquisite froms
and whithers of existence,
                as by shores
soundless, the unspeaking watcher who adores

perceived sails whose mighty brightness dumbs

the utterance of his soul—so even i
wholly chained to a grave astonishment
feel in my being the delirious smart

of thrilled ecstasy, where sea and sky
marry—

  to know the white ship of thy heart

on frailer ports of costlier commerce bent

V

a wind has blown the rain away and blown
the sky away and all the leaves away,
and the trees stand. I think i too have known
autumn too long

    (and what have you to say,
wind wind wind—did you love somebody
and have you the petal of somewhere in your heart
pinched from dumb summer?
      O crazy daddy
of death dance cruelly for us and start

the last leaf whirling in the final brain
of air!) Let us as we have seen see
doom's integration . . . . a wind has blown the rain

away and the leaves and the sky and the
trees stand:
   the trees stand. The trees,
suddenly wait against the moon's face.

V I

a connotation of infinity
sharpens the temporal splendor of this night

when souls which have forgot frivolity
in lowliness, noting the fatal flight
of worlds whereto this earth 's a hurled dream

down eager avenues of lifelessness

consider for how much themselves shall gleam,
in the poised radiance of perpetualness.
When what 's in velvet beyond doomed thought

is like a woman amorous to be known;
and man, whose here is alway worse than naught,
feels the tremendous yonder for his own—

on such a night the sea through her blind miles

of crumbling silence seriously smiles

SONNETS—ACTUALITIES

I

a thing most new complete fragile intense,
which wholly trembling memory undertakes
—your kiss, the little pushings of flesh, makes
my body sorry when the minute moon
is a remarkable splinter in the quick
of twilight
                . . . . or if sunset utters one
unhurried muscled huge chromatic
fist skilfully modeling silence
—to feel how through the stopped entire day
horribly and seriously thrills
the moment of enthusiastic space
is a little wonderful, and say
Perhaps her body touched me; and to face

suddenly the lighted living hills

II

my love is building a building
around you, a frail slippery
house, a strong fragile house
(beginning at the singular beginning

of your smile)a skilful uncouth
prison, a precise clumsy
prison(building thatandthis into Thus,
Around the reckless magic of your mouth)

my love is building a magic, a discrete
tower of magic and(as i guess)

when Farmer Death(whom fairies hate)shall

crumble the mouth-flower fleet
He'll not my tower,
                              laborious, casual

where the surrounded smile
                              hangs

                                             breathless

III

yours is the music for no instrument
yours the preposterous colour unbeheld

—mine the unbought contemptuous intent
till this our flesh merely shall be excelled
by speaking flower
                              (if i have made songs

it does not greatly matter to the sun,
nor will rain care
                              cautiously who prolongs
unserious twilight) shadows have begun

the hair's worm huge, ecstatic, rathe . . . .

yours are the poems i do not write.

In this at least we have got a bulge on death,
silence, and the keenly musical light

of sudden nothing . . . . la bocca mia "he
kissed wholly trembling"

                or so thought the lady.

I V

by little accurate saints thickly which tread
the serene nervous light of paradise—
by angelfaces clustered like bright lice

about god's capable dull important head—
by on whom glories whisperingly impinge
(god's pretty mother)but may not confuse

the clever hair nor rout the young mouth whose
lips begin a smile exactly strange—
this painter should have loved my lady.
And by this throat a little suddenly lifted

in singing—hands fragile whom almost tire
the sleepshaped lilies—

                should my lady's body
with these frail ladies dangerously respire:

impeccable girls in raiment laughter-gifted.

V

notice the convulsed orange inch of moon
perching on this silver minute of evening.

We'll choose the way to the forest—no offense
to you, white town whose spires softly dare.
Will take the houseless wisping rune
of road lazily carved on sharpening air.

Fields lying miraculous in violent silence

fill with microscopic whithering
. . .(that's the Black People, chérie,
who live under stones.) Don't be afraid

and we will pass the simple ugliness
of exact tombs, where a large road crosses
and all the people are minutely dead.

Then you will slowly kiss me

To
E. O.

A

POST IMPRESSIONS

I

windows go orange in the slowly.
town,   night
featherly swifts
the
        Dark on us
all;
        stories told returned

        gather

        the

Again: who

danc   ing
goes utter   ly

churning
witty,twitters

                upon **Our**

(ta-te-ta
in a parenthesis!said the moon

)

I I

riverly is a flower
gone softly by tomb
rosily gods whiten
befall saith rain

anguish
of dream-send is
hushed
in

moan-loll where
night   gathers
morte carved smiles

cloud-gloss is at moon-cease
soon
verbal mist-flowers close
ghosts on prowl gorge

sly slim gods stare

III

the wind is a Lady with
bright slender eyes(who

moves)at sunset
and who—touches—the
hills without any reason

(i have spoken with this
indubitable and green person "Are
You the wind?" "Yes" "why do you touch flowers
as if they were unalive, as

if They were ideas?" "because, sir
things which in my mind blossom will
stumble beneath a clumsiest disguise, appear
capable of fragility and indecision

—do not suppose these
without any reason and otherwise
roses and mountains
different from the i am who wanders

imminently across the renewed world"
to me said the)wind being A lady in a green
dress, who; touches: the fields
(at sunset)

I V

Take for example this:

if to the colour of midnight
to a more than darkness(which
is myself and Paris and all
things)the bright
rain
occurs deeply, beautifully

and i(being at a window
in this midnight)
           for no reason feel
deeply completely conscious of the rain or rather
Somebody who uses roofs and streets skilfully to make a
possible and beautiful sound:

if a(perhaps)clock strikes, in the alive
coolness, very faintly and
finally through altogether delicate gestures of rain

a colour comes, which is morning, O do not wonder that

(just at the edge of day)i surely
make a millionth poem which will not wholly
miss you; or if i certainly create, lady,
one of the thousand selves who are your smile.

V

Paris; this April sunset completely utters
utters serenely silently a cathedral

before whose upward lean magnificent face
the streets turn young with rain,

spiral acres of bloated rose
coiled within cobalt miles of sky
yield to and heed
the mauve
            of twilight(who slenderly descends,
daintily carrying in her eyes the dangerous first stars)
people move love hurry in a gently

arriving gloom and
see!(the new moon
fills abruptly with sudden silver
these torn pockets of lame and begging colour)while
there and here the lithe indolent prostitute
Night, argues

with certain houses

V I

I remark this beach has been used too.   much Too.
originally spontaneous twurls-of-excrement inanely
codified with superb sunlight,   jolts of delapida-
tion bath-houses whose opened withins ejaculate.
obscenity   the tide Did dl es a,fad ed explosion
of, pink!stocking

w h e e saysthesea-brE aking-b Re   akin g(brea)K
ing

my Nose puts on sharp robes of uncouth odour,for an
onion!for one—onion for. putrescence is Cubical
sliced-nicelybits Of, shivers ofcrin Ging stink.dull,
globular glows and flatchatte ringarom a .s

—w hee e;

seasays Break snice-Ly in-twin K les Of,CleaN

a booming smell waddles toward,me,dressed like a
Plum grinning softly,New focus-of disintegrat i o n ?
my

mind laughsin- to Slivers of (unthinking.c'est

l'heure

       exquise)i remind Me of HerThe delicate-swill
tints of hair Whose(the lit-tle m-oo-n' s o u t)
flesh   stalks the Momentinmyarms

your expression
          my love
              when most passionate.,
                      my,love
is thatofa fly.pre cisel Yhalf

(squashe)d

       with,its,little,solemn,   entrails

V I I

my smallheaded pearshaped

lady in gluey twilight
moving, suddenly

is three animals. The
minute waist continually

with an African gesture

utters a frivolous intense half of
Girl which (like some

floating snake upon itself always and
slowly which upward certainly is pouring) emits
a pose
       :to twitter wickedly

whereas the big and firm legs moving solemnly
like careful and furious and beautiful elephants

(mingled in whispering thickly smooth thighs
thinkingly)
remind me of Woman and

how between
her hips India is

VIII

i was sitting in mcsorley's.   outside it was New
York and beautifully snowing.

Inside snug and evil.   the slobbering walls filthily
push witless creases of screaming warmth chuck pillows are noise funnily swallows swallowing revolv-
ingly pompous a the swallowed mottle with smooth
or a but of rapidly goes gobs the and of flecks of and a
chatter sobbings intersect with which distinct disks of
graceful oath, upsoarings the break on   ceiling-
flatness

the Bar.tinking luscious jigs dint of ripe silver with
warmlyish wetflat splurging smells waltz the glush of
squirting taps plus slush of foam knocked off and a
faint piddle-of-drops she says I ploc spittle what the
lands thaz me kid in no sir hopping sawdust you kiddo
he's a palping wreaths of badly Yep cigars who jim
him why gluey grins topple together eyes pout gestures stickily point made glints squinting who's a wink
bum-nothing and money fuzzily mouths take big
wobbly foot-steps every goggle cent of it get out ears
dribbles soft right old feller belch the chap hic sum-
more eh chuckles skulch . . . .

and i was sitting in the din thinking drinking the ale,
which never lets you grow old blinking at the low
ceiling my being pleasantly was punctuated by the always retchings of a worthless lamp.

when With a minute terrif   iceffort one dirty squeal
of soiling light yanKing from bushy obscurity a bald
greenish foetal head established It suddenly upon the
huge neck around whose unwashed sonorous muscle
the filth of a collar hung gently.

(spattered) by this instant of semiluminous nausea A
vast wordless nondescript genie of trunk trickled firmly in to one exactly-mutilated ghost of a chair,

a;domeshaped interval of complete plasticity, shoulders, sprouted the extraordinary arms through an angle of ridiculous velocity commenting upon an un-
clean table.and,whose distended immense Both paws
slowly loved a dinted mug

gone Darkness   it was so near to me, i ask of shadow won't you have a drink?

(the eternal perpetual question)

Inside snugandevil.   i was sitting in mcsorley's
It, did not answer.

outside.(it was New York and beautifully,snowing. . . .

I X

of this sunset(which is so
filled with fear people bells)i
say your eyes can take
day away more softly horribly suddenly;

(of these two most
early stars wincing upon a single
colour, i know only that your hands
move more simply upon the evening

and à propos such light and shape as means
the moon, i somehow feel
your smile slightly is a more
minute adventure)

lady. The clumsy dark threatens(and i do
not speak nor think nor am aware
of anything
         save that these houses bulge
like memories in one crooked street

of a mind peacefully and skilfully which is disappearing

X

SNO

  a white idea(Listen

drenches:earth's ugly)mind.
,Rinsing with exact death

the annual brain
          clotted with loosely voices
look
look. Skilfully

.fingered by(a parenthesis
the)pond on whoseswooning edge

black trees think

(hear little knives of flower
stropping sof a. Thick silence)

blacktreesthink

tiny,angels sharpen:themselves

(on
  air)
don't speak
      A white idea,

drenching. earth's brain detaches
clottingsand from a a nnual(ugliness
of)rinsed mind slowly:

from!the:A wending putrescence. a.of,loosely

;voices

XI

my eyes are fond of the east side
as i lie asleep my eyes go into Allen street the dark
long cool tunnel of raving colour, on either side the
windows are packed with hardslippery greens and
helplessbaby blues and stic-ky chromes and pretty-
lemons and virginal pinks and wealthy vermilion
and breathless-scarlet,dark colours like 'cellos keen
fiddling colours colours cOOler than harps colours
p r i c k i n glike piccolos thumPing colours like a
bangofpiano colours which,are,the,flowery pluckings
of a harpsichord colours of Pure percussion colours-
like-trumpets they(writhe they,struggleinweird chords
of humorous,fury heapingandsqueezing tum-bling-
scratchingcrowd ingworming each by screetching
Each)on either side the street's DarkcOOllonGBody
windows, are. clenched. fists of tint.

    TUMTITUMTIDDLE

if sometimes my eyes stay at home
then my mouth will go out into the East side,my
mouth goes to the peddlers,to the peddlers of smooth,
fruits of eager colours of the little,huddling nuts and
the bad candies my,mouth loves melons slitted with
bright knives,it stains itself,with currants and cherries
it(swallow s bun chesofnew grapes likeGree n
A r e b u b b l e s asc end-ing inthecarts my,mouth
is,fond of tiny plums of tangerines and apples it will,
Gorge indistinct palishflesh of laZilytas tingg OO
seberries,it,loves these better than,cubesandovalsof
sweetness but it swallow) s greedily sugaredellipses
it does not disdain picKles,once,it,ate a scarlet pepper
and my eyes were buttoned with pain

    THE BLACK CAT WITH

is there anything my ears love it's
to go into the east Side in a. dark street a hur-
DygurdY with thequeer hopping ghosts of children. my,ears know the fuZZy tune that's played by
the Funny hand of the paralyticwhose dod d e rin g
partner whEEl shi min chb yi nch along the whirl-
ingPeaceful furious street people drop,coppers into,
the littletin-cup His wrappedupbody Queerly Has,
my,ears,go into Hassan's place the canounchir p ing
the bigtwittering zither-and the mealy,ladies dancing

thicklyfoolish,with,the,tam,bou,rine,s And the violin
spitting squeaky songs into the cuspidor-col ouredRoom
and,my ears bend to the little silent handorgan propping the curve of the tiny motheaten old manwhose
Beard rests.onthetopwhose silly,Hand revolves,per-
fectly,slowlywith,the handle ofa crankin It The L's
roar tortures-pleasantly myears it is,like the,Jab:of a
dark tool. With a cleverjeRk in itlike the motionofa
Sharp Knife-sN ap-ingof fadeadf ish' shead Or,the
whipping of a blackSnake cu tSudden ly in 2 that,
writhes . . . A . .lit.tleora basket of RipeBlackbeRRies
emptied suddenl (y down the squirming sPine of the)
unsuspecting street;
    THE YELLOW EYES AND
—;i Like to
Lie On My Couch at Christopher Street For my
stomach goes out into the east side my sex sitting upright on the stomach like A billiken with hisknees
huggedtogether it,goes out into the rapid hard women and intotheslow hot women   my Stomach
ruBSiTSElf kew-ri-ous-ly a mong Them(among
their stomachs andtheir sexes   )stomachsofold
pe o pleLike hideous vegetaBles weasOned with-be-
ing-put-too-long in windows and never sold and
couldn't-be-given-away because Who?wanted them,
stomachslikEDead fishe s s olemnandputrid vast,
stomachs bLurting and cHuckling like uninteresting-
landscapes made interesting by earTHQuake empty
stomachsClenche Dtothe beautiful-curveofhunger,
cHuBbY stomachs which have not,known other
stomachs and their Sexis a Lone ly,flower whose
secretloveliness hur.ts itse;l.f to no-thing   significant stomachs:Who carry-tadpole!s,,stomachs of little,
girls smoothanduseless i,like,best,the,stomachs,of the
young (girls silky and lewd)like corn s l e n derl y
tottering in sun-light
    THE
nobody(knows and WhoEver would)?dance lewd
dollies pretty and putrid dollies of-love-and-of-death
dollies of perfect life,

dollies of anyway
    VIOLIN

XII

suppose
Life is an old man carrying flowers on his head.

young death sits in a café
smiling, a piece of money held between
his thumb and first finger

(i say "will he buy flowers" to you
and "Death is young
life wears velour trousers
life totters, life has a beard" i

say to you who are silent.—"Do you see
Life? he is there and here,
or that, or this
or nothing or an old man 3 thirds
asleep, on his head
flowers, always crying
to nobody something about les
roses les bluets
                    yes,
                         will He buy?
Les belles bottes—oh hear
, pas chères")

and my love slowly answered I think so.   But
I think I see someone else

there is a lady, whose name is Afterwards
she is sitting beside young death, is slender;
likes flowers.

XIII

the dress was a suspicious madder, importing the cruelty of roses.
The exciting simplicity of her hipless body, pausing to invent imperceptible bulgings of the pretended breasts, forked in surprisable
unliving eyes chopped by a swollen inanity of picture hat.
    the arms hung ugly., the hands sharp and impertinently dead.

expression began with the early cessation of her skirt. fleshless melody of the, keenly lascivious legs. painful ankles large acute brutal feet propped on irrelevantly ferocious heels.

Her gasping slippery body moved with the hideous spontaneity of a solemn mechanism. beneath her drab tempo of hasteful futility lived brilliantly the enormous rhythm of absurdity.

skin like the poisonous fragility of ice newly formed upon an old pool. Her nose was small, exact, stupid. mouth normal, large, unclever. hair genuinely artificial, unpleasantly tremendous.

under flat lusts of light her nice concupiscence appeared rounded.

if she were alive, death was amusing

XIV

inthe,exquisite;

morning   sure   lyHer eye s exactly sit,ata little roundtable among otherlittle roundtables Her,eyes   count slow(ly

obstre poroustimidi ties surElyfl)oat iNg,the

ofpieces ofof sunligh tof fa l l in gof throughof treesOf.

(Fields Elysian

the like,a)slEEping neck a breathing a   ,lies
(slo wlythe wom an pa)ris her
flesh:wakes
               in little streets

while exactlygir lisHlegs;play;ing;nake;D
and

chairs wait under the trees

Fields slowly Elysian in

a firmcool-Ness   taxis, s.QuirM

and,   b etw ee nch air st ott er s thesillyold
WomanSellingBalloonS

In theex qui site

morning,
          her sureLyeye s sit-ex actly her sitsat a surely!little,
roundtable amongother;littleexactly round.   tables,

Her
     .eyes

PORTRAITS

I

being
twelve
who hast merely
gonorrhea

                    Oldeyed
child, to
ambitious weeness
of boots

tiny
add
death
what

shall?

I I

Babylon slim
-ness of
evenslicing
eyes are chisels

scarlet Goes
with her
whitehot
face,gashed

by hair's blue cold

jolts of
lovecrazed abrupt

flesh split "Pretty
Baby"
to
numb rhythm before christ

I I I

ta
ppin
g
toe

hip
popot
amus Back

gen
teel-ly
lugu-
bri ous

                           eyes
LOOPTHELOOP

as

fathandsbangrag

I V

the waddling
madam star
taps
taps.   "ready girls".   the

unspontaneous streets
make bright their eyes
a
blind irisher fiddles a

scotch jig in a stinking
joyman bar
a cockney is
buying whiskies for a turk

a waiter intones:bloo-moo-n
sirkusricky
platzburg
hoppytoad   yesmam.   the

furious taximan
p(ee)ps
on his whistle somebody
says here's luck

somebody else says down the hatch
the nigger smiles
the jew stands
beside his teddy-bears

the sailor shuffles the
night with φυχιυγ eyes
the great black preacher gargles jesus
the aesthete indulges

his soul for certain things which died
it is eighteen hundred
years. . . .
exactly

    under the window
    under the window
    under the window walk

the unburied feet of
the little ladies more than dead

V

raise the shade
will youse dearie?
rain
wouldn't that

get yer goat but
we don't care do
we dearie we should
worry about the rain

huh
dearie?
yknow
i'm

sorry for awl the
poor girls that
gets up god
knows when every

day of their
lives
aint you,
                        oo-oo.   dearie

not so
hard dear

you're killing me

V I

Cleopatra built
like a smooth arrow or
a fleet pillar is eaten
by yesterday

she was a silver tube of wise
lust whose arms and legs
like white squirming pipes
wiggle upon the perfumed roman

strength who how
furiously plays the hot
sweet horrible stops of
her

body
Cleopatra had a
body
it was

thick slim warm moist
built like an organ
and it
loved

he
was a roman   theirs was a
music sinuous globular
slippery intense witty huge

and its chords
brittle eager eternal luminous
firmly diminishing have swoopingly
fallen svelte sagging gone into the soaring silence

(put
your smallest
ear against yester-
day My Lady   hear

the purple trumpets
blow   horses of gold
delicately crouching beneath silver
youths   the leaneyed

Caesars borne neatly through enormous
twilight surrounded by their triumphs
and
     listen well

how the dainty destroyed
hero clamps the hearty sharp
column
of Egypt

        ,built like a fleet
pillar or a smooth
arrow
Cleopatra is eaten by

yester-
day)
     O i tell you out of
the minute incessant Was irrevocably

emanates a dignity of papyruscoloured
faces   superbly limp
the ostensible centuries
therefore let us be

a little uncouth and amorous in
memory of Cleopatra and of
Antony
and we will

confuse hotly our moreover irrevocable
bodies while the infinite processions
move like moths and like boys and
like incense and like sunlight

and like ships and like young girls and like
butterflies and like money
and like laughter
and like elephants

through our
single
brain   in memory of Cleopatra   while
easily

tremendously
floats
in the bright shouting street of time
her nakedness with its blue hair

(all is eaten by yester-
day
between the nibbling timid teethful hours
wilts the stern texture of Now

the arrow and the
pillar pursue curiously
a crumbling flight into the absolute stars
the gods are swallowed

even
Nile
the
kind black great god)

Cleopatra you
are eaten
by yester-
day

(and O My Lady Lady Of
Ladies you
who move beautifully in the winds
of my lust like a high troubling

ship upon the fragrant
unspeaking ignorant darkness of New
Lady whose kiss is
a procession of deep beasts

coming with keen ridiculous
silks coming with sharp languid perfumes
coming with the little profound gems and
the large laughing stones

a sinuous problem of colour
floating against
the clever deadly
heaven   i salute

you
whose body is
Egypt
whose hair is Nile)

put your ear
to the ground
there is a music
Lady

          the noiseless truth of swirling
worms
is
tomorrow

VII

between the breasts
of bestial
Marj lie large
men who praise

Marj's cleancornered strokable
body   these men's
fingers toss trunks
shuffle sacks spin kegs they

curl
loving
around
beers

the world has
these men's hands but their
bodies big and boozing
belong to

Marj
the greenslim purse of whose
face opens
on a fatgold

grin
hooray
hoorah for the large
men who lie

between the breasts
of bestial Marj
for the strong men
who

sleep between the legs of Lil

VIII

when the spent day begins to frail
(whose grave already three or two
young stars with spades of silver dig)

by beauty i declare to you

if what i am at one o'clock
to little lips(which have not sinned
in whose displeasure lives a kiss)
kneeling, your frequent mercy begs,

sharply believe me, wholly, well
—did(wisely suddenly into
a dangerous womb of cringing air)
the largest hour push deep his din

of wallowing male(shock beyond shock
blurted)strokes, vibrant with the purr
of echo pouring in a mesh
of following tone: did this and this

spire strike midnight(and did occur
bell beyond fiercely spurting bell
a jetted music splashing fresh
upon silence)i without fail

entered became and was these twin
imminent lisping bags of flesh;
became eyes moist lithe shuddering big,
the luminous laughter, and the legs

whereas, at twenty minutes to

one, i am this blueeyed Finn
emerging from a lovehouse who
buttons his coat against the wind

IX

impossibly

motivated by midnight
the flyspecked abdominous female
indubitably tellurian
strolls
        emitting minute grins

each an intaglio.
Nothing
has also carved upon her much

too white forehead a pair of
eyes which mutter thickly(as one merely
terricolous American an instant doubts
the authenticity

of these antiquities—relaxing
                              hurries
elsewhere; to blow

incredible wampum

                    X

here is little Effie's head
whose brains are made of gingerbread
when the judgment day comes
God will find six crumbs

stooping by the coffinlid
waiting for something to rise
as the other somethings did—
you imagine His surprise

bellowing through the general noise
Where is Effie who was dead?
—to God in a tiny voice,
i am may the first crumb said

whereupon its fellow five
crumbs chuckled as if they were alive
and number two took up the song,
might i'm called and did no wrong

cried the third crumb, i am should
and this is my little sister could
with our big brother who is would
don't punish us for we were good;

and the last crumb with some shame
whispered unto God, my name
is must and with the others i've
been Effie who isn't alive

just imagine it I say
God amid a monstrous din
watch your step and follow me
stooping by Effie's little, in

(want a match or can you see?)
which the six subjunctive crumbs
twitch like mutilated thumbs:
picture His peering biggest whey

coloured face on which a frown
puzzles, but I know the way—
(nervously Whose eyes approve
the blessed while His ears are crammed

with the strenuous music of
the innumerable capering damned)
—staring wildly up and down
the here we are now judgment day

cross the threshold have no dread
lift the sheet back in this way.
here is little Effie's head
whose brains are made of gingerbread

XI

her
flesh
Came
at

meassandca V
               ingint
                         oA
chute

    i had cement for her,
    merrily
we became each
other humped to tumbling

```
garble     when
a
minute
pulled the sluice
```

emerging.

concrete

XII

little ladies more
than dead exactly dance
in my head, precisely
dance where danced la guerre.

Mimi à
la voix fragile
qui chatouille Des
Italiens

the putain with the ivory throat
Marie Louise Lallemand
n'est-ce pas que je suis belle
chéri? les anglais m'aiment
tous, les américains
aussi . . . . "bon dos, bon cul de Paris"(Marie
Vierge
Priez
Pour
Nous)

with the
long lips of
Lucienne which dangle
the old men and hot
men se promènent
doucement le soir(ladies

accurately dead les anglais
sont gentils et les américains
aussi, ils payent bien les américains dance
exactly in my brain voulez-
vous coucher avec
moi? Non? pourquoi?)

ladies skilfully
dead precisely dance
where has danced la
guerre j'm'appelle
Manon, cinq rue Henri Mounier
voulez-vous coucher avec moi?
te ferai Mimi
te ferai Minette,
dead exactly dance
si vous voulez
chatouiller
mon lézard ladies suddenly
j'm'en fous des nègres

                      (in the twilight of Paris
Marie Louise with queenly
legs cinq rue Henri
Mounier a little love
begs, Mimi with the body
like une boite à joujoux, want nice sleep?
toutes les petites femmes exactes
qui dansent toujours in my
head dis-donc, Paris

ta gorge mystérieuse
pourquoi se promène-t-elle, pourquoi
éclate ta voix
fragile couleur de pivoine?)
                         with the

long lips of Lucienne which
dangle the old men and hot men
precisely dance in my head
ladies carefully dead

N

&: SEVEN POEMS

I

                        i will be
M o ving in the Street of her

bodyfee l inga ro undMe the traffic of
lovely;muscles-sinke x p i r i n g S
     uddenl
Y   totouch
               the curvedship of
                              Her-
. . . .kIss   her:hands
                    will play on,mE as
dea d tunes OR s-cra p-y leaVes flut te rin g
from Hideous trees or

     Maybe Mandolins
                    l oo k-
     pigeons fly ingand

whee(:are,SpRiN,k,LiNg an in-stant with sunLight
t h e n)l-
ing all go BlacK wh-eel-ing

oh
   ver
       mYveRylitTle

street
where
you will come,

               at twi li ght
     s(oon & there's
     a   m oo
)n.

II

i'll tell you a dream i had once i was away up in the
sky Blue,everything:a bar the bar was made of brass
hangIng from strings (or)someThing i was lying on
the bar it was cOOl i didn't have anything on and I
was hot all Hot and the bar was

    COOl
O My lover,

                  there's just room for me in You
my stomach goes into your Little Stomach My legs
are in your legs Your arms
                        under me around; my head
fits(my head)in your Brain —my, head's
big
she(said laughing
)with your head.all big

III

Spring is like a perhaps hand
(which comes carefully
out of Nowhere)arranging
a window,into which people look(while
people stare
arranging and changing placing
carefully there a strange
thing and a known thing here)and

changing everything carefully

spring is like a perhaps
Hand in a window
(carefully to
and fro moving New and
Old things,while
people stare carefully
moving a perhaps
fraction of flower here placing
an inch of air there)and

without breaking anything.

IV

Who
       threw the silver dollar up into the tree?
                                             I didn't
said the little lady who sews and grows every day
paler-paler she sits sewing and growing and that's the
truth,
who threw

         the ripe melon into the tree?you
                                 got me
said the smoke who runs the elevator but I bet two bits
come seven come eleven m m make the world safe for
democracy it never fails and that's a fact;

who threw the

bunch of violets
               into the tree?I dunno said the silver
dog, with ripe eyes and wagged his tail that's the
god's own

and the moon kissed the little lady on her paler-paler
face and said never mind,you'll find
                          But the moon
creeped into the pink hand of the smoke that shook
the ivories
            and she said said She Win and you won't
be sorry   And The Moon came!along-along to the
waggy silver dog
and the moon came
and the Moon said into his Ripe Eyes
                        and the moon
  Smiled
, so

V

gee i like to think of dead it means nearer because deeper
firmer since darker than little round water at one end of
the well   it's too cool to be crooked and it's too firm
to be hard but it's sharp and thick and it loves,   every
old thing falls in rosebugs and jackknives and kittens and

pennies they all sit there looking at each other having the
fastest time because they've never met before

dead's more even than how many ways of sitting on
your head your unnatural hair has in the morning

dead's clever too like POF goes the alarm off and the
little striker having the best time tickling away everybody's brain so everybody just puts out their finger
and they stuff the poor thing all full of fingers

dead has a smile like the nicest man you've never met
who maybe winks at you in a streetcar and you pretend
you don't but really you do see and you are My how
glad he winked and hope he'll do it again

or if it talks about you somewhere behind your back it
makes your neck feel pleasant and stoopid   and if
dead says may i have this one and was never intro-
duced you say Yes because you know you want it to
dance with you and it wants to and it can dance and
Whocares

dead's fine like hands do you see that water flowerpots
in windows but they live higher in their house than
you so that's all you see but you don't want to

dead's happy like the way underclothes All so differently solemn and inti and sitting on one string

dead never says my dear,Time for your musiclesson
and you like music and to have somebody play who
can but you know you never can and why have to?

dead's nice like a dance where you danced simple hours
and you take all your prickley-clothes off and squeeze-
into-largeness without one word   and you lie still as
anything   in largeness and this largeness begins to
give you,the dance all over again and you,feel all again
all over the way men you liked made you feel when they
touched you(but that's not all)because largeness tells
you so you can feel what you made,men feel when,you
touched,them

dead's sorry like a thistlefluff-thing which goes landing away all by himself on somebody's roof or something where who-ever-heard-of-growing and nobody
expects you to anyway

dead says come with me he says(andwhyevernot)into
the round well and see the kitten and the penny and
the jackknife and the rosebug

                    and you say Sure you
say (like that) sure i'll come with you you say for i
like kittens i do and jackknives i do and pennies i do
and rosebugs i do

V I

        (one!)

the wisti-twisti barber
-pole is climbing

people high,up-in

tenements talk.in sawdust Voices

                  a:whispering drunkard passes

V I I

who knows if the moon's
a balloon,coming out of a keen city
in the sky—filled with pretty people?
(and if you and i should

get into it,if they
should take me and take you into their balloon,
why then
we'd go up higher with all the pretty people

than houses and steeples and clouds:
go sailing
away and away sailing into a keen
city which nobody's ever visited,where

always
      it's
          Spring)and everyone's
in love and flowers pick themselves

D

SONNETS—REALITIES

I

O It's Nice To Get Up In,the slipshod mucous kiss
of her riant belly's fooling bore
—When The Sun Begins To(with a phrasing crease
of hot subliminal lips,as if a score
of youngest angels suddenly should stretch neat necks
just to see how always squirms
the skilful mystery of Hell)me suddenly

grips in chuckles of supreme sex.

In The Good Old Summer Time.
My gorgeous bullet in tickling intuitive flight
aches,just,simply,into,her.   Thirsty
stirring.   (Must be summer.   Hush.   Worms.)
But It's Nicer To Lie In Bed
                              —eh?   I'm

not.   Again.   Hush.   God.   Please hold.   Tight

II

my strength becoming wistful in a glib

girl i consider her as a leaf
                              thinks
of the sky,my mind takes to nib
-bling,of her posture.   (As an eye winks).

and almost i refrain from jumbling her
flesh whose casual mouth's coy rooting
dies also.   (my loveFist in her knuckling

thighs,
     with a sharp indecent stir
unclenches

        into fingers. . . .she too is tired.
Not of me.   The eyes which biggish loll

the hands' will tumbling into shall

—and Love 's a coach with gilt hopeless wheels mired
where sits rigidly her body's doll
gay exactly perishing sexual,

I I I

the dirty colours of her kiss have just
throttled
       my seeing blood,her heart's chatter

riveted a weeping skyscraper

in me

     i bite on the eyes' brittle crust
(only feeling the belly's merry thrust
Boost my huge passion like a business

and the Y her legs panting as they press

proffers its omelet of fluffy lust)
at six exactly
       the alarm tore

two slits in her cheeks. A brain peered at the dawn.
she got up

      with a gashing yellow yawn
and tottered to a glass bumping things.
she picked wearily something from the floor

Her hair was mussed,and she coughed while tying strings

I V

light cursed falling in a singular block
her,rain-warm-naked

               exquisitely hashed

(little careful hunks-of-lilac laughter splashed
from the world prettily upward,mock
us . . . .)
         and there was a clock. tac-tic. tac-toc.

Time and lilacs. . . .minutes and love. . . .do you?and
always
      (i simply understand
the gnashing petals of sex which lock
me seriously.

          Dumb for a while.my

god—a patter of kisses,the chewed stump

of a mouth,huge dropping of a flesh from
hinging thighs
           . . . .merci. . . .i want to die
nous sommes heureux

            my soul a limp lump

of lymph
     she kissed
        and i

           . . . .chéri. . . .nous sommes

V

    the bed is not very big

    a sufficient pillow shoveling
    her small manure-shaped head

    one sheet on which distinctly wags

at times the weary twig
of a neckless nudity
(very occasionally budding

a flabby algebraic odour

jigs
        et tout en face
always wiggles the perfectly dead
finger of thitherhithering gas.

clothed with a luminous fur

poilu

        a Jesus sags
in frolicsome wooden agony).

V I

the poem her belly marched through me as
one army. From her nostrils to her feet

she smelled of silence. The inspired cleat

of her glad leg pulled into a sole mass
my separate lusts
                her hair was like a gas
evil to feel. Unwieldy . . . .

                        the bloodbeat
in her fierce laziness tried to repeat
a trick of syncopation Europe has

—. One day i felt a mountain touch me where
i stood(maybe nine miles off). It was spring

sun-stirring. sweetly to the mangling air
muchness of buds mattered. a valley spilled
its tickling river in my eyes,
                        the killed

world wriggled like a twitched string.

VII

an amiable putrescence carpenters

the village of her mind bodily which

ravelling,to a proud continual stitch
of the unmitigated sistole
                              purrs
against my mind,the eyes' shuddering burrs
of light stick on my brain harder than can twitch
its terrors;
            the,mouth's,swallowed,muscle(itch
of groping mucous)in my mouth occurs

homelessly. While grip Hips simply. well
fussed flesh does surely to mesh. New
and eager. wittily peels the. ploop. —OOc h get:breath
once,all over,kid how,funny Do tell
. . . . sweat,succeeds breathings stopped
                                        to

hear,in darkness,water the lips of death

VIII

her careful distinct sex whose sharp lips comb

my mumbling gropeofstrength(staggered by the lug
of love)
        sincerely greets,with an occult shrug
asking Through her Muteness will slowly roam
my dumbNess?

                her other,wet,warm

lips limp,across my bruising smile;
as rapidly upon the jiggled norm

of agony my grunting eyes pin tailored flames
Her being at this instant commits

an impenetrable transparency.
the harsh erecting breasts and uttering tits
punish my hug
                    presto!

                            the bright rile
of jovial hair extremely frames

the face in a hoop of grim ecstasy

I X

irreproachable ladies firmly lewd
on dangerous slabs of tilting din whose
mouths distinctly walk
                    your smiles accuse

the dusk with an untimid svelte subdued
magic
            while in your eyes there lives
a green egyptian noise. ladies with whom time

feeds especially his immense lips

On whose deep nakedness death most believes,
perpetual girls marching to love

whose bodies kiss me with the square crime
of life . . . . Cecile, the oval shove
of hiding pleasure. Alice, stinging quips
of flesh. Loretta, cut the comedy
kid . . . .

        Fran Mag Glad Dorothy

X

nearer:breath of my breath:take not thy tingling
limbs from me:make my pain their crazy meal
letting thy tigers of smooth sweetness steal
slowly in dumb blossoms of new mingling:
deeper:blood of my blood:with upwardcringing
swiftness plunge these leopards of white dream
in the glad flesh of my fear:more neatly ream
this pith of darkness:carve an evilfringing
flower of madness on gritted lips
and on sprawled eyes squirming with light insane
chisel the killing flame that dizzily grips.

Querying greys between mouthed houses curl

thirstily. Dead stars stink. dawn. Inane,

the poetic carcass of a girl

XI

god pity me whom(god distinctly has)
the weightless svelte drifting sexual feather
of your shall i say body?follows
truly through a dribbling moan of jazz

whose arched occasional steep youth swallows
curvingly the keenness of my hips;
or, your first twitch of crisp boy flesh dips
my height in a firm fragile stinging weather,

(breathless with sharp necessary lips)kid

female cracksman of the nifty,ruffian-rogue,
laughing body with wise breasts half-grown,
lisping flesh quick to thread the fattish drone
of I Want a Doll,
                              wispish-agile feet with slid
steps parting the tousle of saxophonic brogue.

XII

even a pencil has fear to
do the posed body luckily made
a pen is dreadfully afraid
of her of this of the smile's two
eyes. . . .too,since the world's but
a piece of eminent fragility.
Well and when—Does susceptibility
imply perspicuity,or?
                              shut
up.
    Seeing
            seeing her is not
to something or to nothing as much as
being by her seen,which has got
nothing on something as i think

,did you ever hear a jazz
Band?

        or unnoise men don't make soup who drink.

XIII

unnoticed woman from whose kind large flesh

i turn to the cruel-littleness of cold
(when battling street-lamps fail upon the gold
dawn, where teeth of slowturning streets mesh

in a frieze of smoking Face Bluish-old

and choked pat of going solès on flat
pavements with icy cries of this and that
stumbling in gloom, bad laughters, smiles unbold)

also, tomorrow the daily papers will feature
Peace And Good Will, and Mary with one lung
extended to the pumping Child, and " 'Twas

the night before Christmas when all through the house not a creature
was stirring, not even a mouse. The stockings were hung
by the chimney with care in hopes that Saint Nicholas"

XIV

she sits dropping on a caret of clenched arms
a delicately elephantine face
(It is necessary to find Hassan's Place
by tiny streets shrugging with colour)
the mouth who sits between her cheeks
utters a thud of scarlet. always. More
interesting, as i think, her charms
en repos . . . . a fattish leg leaks
obscenely from the dress. one nipple tries.
playfully to peek into the belly
whose deep squirm nibbles. another couches,
weary, upon a flabby mattress of jelly . . . .
than when to the canoun she totters, slouches,
with giggling hips and frozen eyes

XV

of this wilting wall the colour drub
souring sunbeams, of a foetal fragrance
to rickety unclosed blinds inslants
peregrinate, a cigar-stub
disintegrates, above, underdrawers club
the faintly sweating air with pinkness,
one pale dog behind a slopcaked shrub
painstakingly utters a slippery mess,
a star sleepily, feebly, scratches the sore
of morning. But i am interested more
intricately in the delicate scorn
with which in a putrid window every day
almost leans a lady whose still-born
smile involves the comedy of decay,

XVI

it started when Bill's chip let on to
the bulls he'd bumped a bloke back in fifteen.
Then she came toward him on her knees across the locked
room. he knocked her cold and beat it for Chicago.

Eddie was waiting for him, and they cleaned up a few
times—before she got the info
from a broad that knew Eddie in Topeka, went clean
daffy, and which was very silly hocked

the diamond he gave her. Bill was put wise
that she was coming with his kid inside her.
He laughed. She came. he gave her a shove
and asked Eddie did he care to ride her?
. . . . she exactly lay, looking hunks of love

in The Chair he kept talking about eyes

XVII

whereas by dark really released, the modern
flame of her indomitable body
uses a careful fierceness. Her lips study
my head gripping for a decision: burn
the terrific fingers which grapple and joke
on my passionate anatomy
oh yes! Large legs pinch, toes choke—
hair-thin strands of magic agony
. . . . by day this lady in her limousine

oozes in fashionable traffic, just
a halfsmile (for society's sweet sake)
in the not too frail lips almost discussed;
between her and ourselves a nearly-opaque
perfume disinterestedly obscene.

XVIII

my girl's tall with hard long eyes
as she stands, with her long hard hands keeping
silence on her dress, good for sleeping
is her long hard body filled with surprise
like a white shocking wire, when she smiles
a hard long smile it sometimes makes
gaily go clean through me tickling aches,
and the weak noise of her eyes easily files
my impatience to an edge—my girl's tall
and taut, with thin legs just like a vine
that's spent all of its life on a garden-wall,
and is going to die. When we grimly go to bed
with these legs she begins to heave and twine
about me, and to kiss my face and head.

XIX

in making Marjorie god hurried
a boy's body on unsuspicious
legs of girl. his left hand quarried
the quartzlike face. his right slapped
the amusing big vital vicious
vegetable of her mouth.
Upon the whole he suddenly clapped
a tiny sunset of vermouth
-colour. Hair. he put between
her lips a moist mistake,whose fragrance hurls
me into tears,as the dusty new-
ness of her obsolete gaze begins to. lean . . . .
a little against me,when for two
dollars i fill her hips with boys and girls

XX

Dick Mid's large bluish face without eyebrows

sits in the kitchen nights and chews a two-bit
cigar
        waiting for the bulls to pull his joint.
Jimmie was a dude. Dark hair and nice hands.

with a little eye that rolled and made its point

Jimmie's sister worked for Dick.   And had some rows
over percent.   The gang got shot up twice, it
operated in the hundred ands

All the chips would kid Jimmie to give them a kiss
but Jimmie lived regular.   stewed three times a week.
and slept twice a week with a big toothless girl
in Yonkers.
                    Dick Mid's green large three teeth leak

smoke:remembering, two pink big lips curl . . . .

how Jimmie was framed and got his

XXI

twentyseven bums give a prostitute the once
-over.   fiftythree (and one would see if it could)

eyes say the breasts look very good:
firmlysquirmy with a slight jounce,

thirteen pants have a hunch

admit in threedimensional distress
these hips were made for Horizontal Business
(set on big legs nice to pinch

assiduously which justgraze
each other).   As the lady lazily struts
                                        (her
thickish flesh superior to the genuine daze
of unmarketable excitation,

whose careless movements carefully scatter

pink propaganda of annihilation

XXII

life boosts herself rapidly at me

through sagging debris of exploded day
the hulking perpendicular mammal
                                        a
grim epitome of chuckling flesh.
Weak thirsty fists of idiot futures bash

the bragging breasts,
                        puppy-faces to mouth
her ugly nipples squirming in pretty wrath,
gums skidding on slippery udders

                                    she
lifts an impertinent puerperal face
and with astute fatuous swallowed eyes
smiles,
        one grin very distinctly wobbles
from the thinning lips me hugely which embrace.
as in the hairy notching of clenched thighs

a friendless dingy female frenzy bubbles

SONNETS—ACTUALITIES

I

when my love comes to see me it's
just a little like music, a
little more like curving colour (say
orange)
        against silence, or darkness . . . .

the coming of my love emits
a wonderful smell in my mind,

you should see when i turn to find
her how my least heart-beat becomes less.
And then all her beauty is a vise

whose stilling lips murder suddenly me,

but of my corpse the tool her smile makes something
suddenly luminous and precise

—and then we are I and She . . . .

what is that the hurdy-gurdy's playing

II

    it is funny, you will be dead some day.
    By you the mouth hair eyes, and i mean
    the unique and nervously obscene

    need; it's funny. They will all be dead

    knead of lustfulhunched deeplytoplay
    lips and stare the gross fuzzy-pash
    —dead—and the dark gold delicately smash . . . .
    grass, and the stars, of my shoulder in stead.

    It is a funny, thing. And you will be

    and i and all the days and nights that matter
    knocked by sun moon jabbed jerked with ecstasy
    . . . . tremble (not knowing how much better

    than me will you like the rain's face and

    the rich improbable hands of the Wind)

III

i have loved, let us see if that's all.
Bit into you as teeth, in the stone
of a musical fruit. My lips pleasantly groan
on your taste. Jumped the quick wall

of your smile into stupid gardens
if this were not enough (not really enough
pulled one before one the vague tough

exquisite

        flowers, whom hardens
richly, darkness. On the whole
possibly have i loved . . . . ? you)
                                    sheath before sheath

stripped to the Odour. (and here's what WhoEver will know
Had you as bite teeth;
i stood with you as a foal

stands but as the trees, lay, which grow

I V

        utterly and amusingly i am pash
        possibly because
                        .dusk and if it
        perhaps drea-mingly Is (not-
        quite trees hugging with the rash,
        coherent light
) only to trace with
        stiffening slow shrill eyes beyond a fit-
        and-cling of stuffs the alert willing myth
        of body, which will make oddly to strut
        my indolent priceless smile,
                         until
        this very frail enormous star (do you see
        it?) and this shall dance upon the nude
        and final silence and shall the
        (i do but touch you) timid lewd
        moon plunge skilfully into the hill.

V

        before the fragile gradual throne of night
        slowly when several stars are opening
        one beyond one immaculate curving
        cool treasures of silence
                       (slenderly wholly
        rising, herself uprearing wholly slowly,
        lean in the hips and her sails filled with dream—
        when on a green brief gesture of twilight
        trembles the imagined galleon of Spring)

somewhere unspeaking sits my life; the grim
clenched mind of me somewhere begins again,
shares the year's perfect agony. Waiting

(always) upon a fragile instant when

herself me (slowly, wholly me) will press
in the young lips unearthly slenderness

VI

when i have thought of you somewhat too
much and am become perfectly and
simply Lustful. . . .sense a gradual stir
of beginning muscle, and what it will do
to me before shutting. . . .understand
i love you. . . .feel your suddenly body reach
for me with a speed of white speech

(the simple instant of perfect hunger
Yes)
        how beautifully swims
the fooling world in my huge blood,
cracking brains A swiftlyenormous light
—and furiously puzzling through, prismatic, whims,
the chattering self perceives with hysterical fright

a comic tadpole wriggling in delicious mud

VII

autumn is: that between there and here
gladness flays hideously hills.
It was in the spring of this very year

(a spring of wines women and window-sills)
i met that hideous gladness, per the face
—pinxit, who knows? Who knows? Some "allemand" . . . . ?
of Goethe, since exempt from heaven's grace,

in an engraving belonging to my friend.
Whom i salute, by what is dear to us;
and by a gestured city stilled in the framing
twilight of Spring . . . . and the dream of dreaming
—and i fall back, quietly amorous
of, through the autumn indisputably roaming

death's big rotten particular kiss.

VIII

fabulous against   ,a,fathoming jelly
of vital futile huge light as she
does not stand-ing.unsits

                     her(wrist
performs a thundering trivial)it.y

protuberant through the room's skilful of thing
silent spits discrete lumps of noise . . . .
furniture

        unsolemnly :bur   sting
the skinfull of Ludicrous,solidity which a. ,kissed
with is nearness.(peers:body of

                      aching toys
in unsmooth sexual luminosity spree.

—dear)the   uncouthly Her.thuglike stare the
pollenizing vacancy
when,Thy patters?hands . . . . is swig

it does who eye   sO neatly big

IX

let's live suddenly without thinking

under honest trees,
                    a stream
does. the brain of cleverly-crinkling
-water pursues the angry dream
of the shore. By midnight,
                        a moon
scratches the skin of the organised hills

an edged nothing begins to prune

let's live like the light that kills
and let's as silence,
                        because Whirl's after all:
(after me) love, and after you.
I occasionally feel vague how
vague i don't know tenuous Now-
spears and The Then-arrows making do
our mouths something red, something tall

X

if i should sleep with a lady called death
get another man with firmer lips
to take your new mouth in his teeth
(hips pumping pleasure into hips).

Seeing how the limp huddling string
of your smile over his body squirms
kissingly, i will bring you every spring
handfuls of little normal worms.

Dress deftly your flesh in stupid stuffs,
phrase the immense weapon of your hair.
Understanding why his eye laughs,
i will bring you every year

something which is worth the whole,
an inch of nothing for your soul.

XI

my naked lady framed
in twilight is an accident

whose niceness betters easily the intent
of genius—
            painting wholly feels ashamed
before this music, and poetry cannot
go near because perfectly fearful.

meanwhile these speak her wonderful
But i (having in my arms caught

the picture) hurry it slowly

to my mouth, taste the accurate demure
ferocious
            rhythm of
                        precise
laziness. Eat the price

of an imaginable gesture

exact warm unholy

XII

i have found what you are like
the rain,

        (Who feathers frightened fields
with the superior dust-of-sleep. wields

easily the pale club of the wind
and swirled justly souls of flower strike

the air in utterable coolness

deeds of green thrilling light
                        with thinned

newfragile yellows

                    lurch and.press
—in the woods
          which
               stutter
                   and

                        sing
And the coolness of your smile is
stirringofbirds between my arms; but
i should rather than anything
have (almost when hugeness will shut
quietly) almost,
                 your kiss

XIII

upon the room's
            silence, i will sew

a nagging button of candlelight
(halfstooping to exactly kiss the trite

worm of her nakedness
               until it go

rapidly to bed: i will get in with
it, wisely, pester skilfully, teasing
its lips, absurd eyes, the hair). Creasing
its smoothness—and leave the bed agrin with

memories
         (this white worm and i who

love to feel what it will do
in my bullying fingers)
as for the candle, it'll

turn into a little curse

of wax. Something, distinct and. Amusing, brittle

XIV

the ivory performing rose

of you, worn upon my mind
all night, quitting only in the unkind

dawn its muscle amorous

pricks with minute odour these gross
days
         when i think of you and do not live:
and the empty twilight cannot grieve
nor the autumn, as i grieve, faint for your face

O stay with me slightly.   or until

with neat obscure obvious hands

Time stuff the sincere stomach of each mill

of the ingenious gods. (i am punished.
They have stolen into recent lands
the flower
           with their enormous fingers unwished

XV

(the phonograph's voice like a keen spider skipping

quickly over patriotic swill.
The,negress,in the,rocker by the,curb,tipping

and tipping,the flocks of pigeons.   And the skil-

ful loneliness,and the rather fat
man in bluishsuspenders half-reading the
Evening Something
                    in the normal window.   and a cat.

A cat waiting for god knows makes me

wonder if i'm alive(eye pries,

not open.   Tail stirs.)   And the.fire-escapes—
the night.makes me wonder if,if i am
the face of a baby smeared with beautiful jam

or

    my invincible Nearness rapes

laughter from your preferable,eyes

XVI

    a blue woman with sticking out breasts hanging
clothes. On the line. not so old
for the mother of twelve undershirts(we are told
by is it Bishop Taylor who needs hanging

that marriage is a sure cure for masturbation).

    A dirty wind,twitches the,clothes which are clean
—this is twilight,
              a little puppy hopping between
skipping
     children
           (It is the consumation
of day,the hour)she says to me you big fool
she says i says to her i says Sally
i says
    the

      mmmoon,begins to,drool

softly,in the hot alley,

a nigger's voice feels curiously cool
(suddenly-Lights go!on,by schedule

XVII

let us tremble)a personal radiance sits
hideously upon the trafficing hum
of dusk
      each street takes of shadowy
light the droll snowing delirium

(we do not speak)
                tumbled hushingly bits
of downward flower flowing without or cease

or time; a naming stealth of ecstasy
means, like a girl lasciviously frail,
                              peace
(dreaming is better)

                murdering coolness slowly
in peopling places seeks play:withs of star
link clauses of warmth
                (after dream who knows?)
a blackish cat and a bluish cat are

eyeing, as with almost melancholy
delicacy night gargles windows.

XVIII

      —G O N splashes-sink
which is west eighth, a star or three annoys

me, but the stink of perfumed noise
fiercely mounts from the fireman's ball, i think

and also i think of you, getting mandolin-clink
mixed with your hair; feeling your knees
among the supercilious chimneys,

my nerves sumptuously wink
. . . . and little-dusk has his toys to play with
windows-and-whispers,
                (will BigMorning get away with
them? j'm'en doute,)
          chérie, j'm'en doute.

the accurate key to a palace

—You,—in this window sits a Face
(it is twilight)a Face playing on a flute

XIX

the mind is its own beautiful prisoner.
Mine looked long at the sticky moon
opening in dusk her new wings

then decently hanged himself, one afternoon.

The last thing he saw was you
naked amid unnaked things,

your flesh, a succinct wandlike animal,
a little strolling with the futile purr
of blood; your sex squeaked like a billiard-cue
chalking itself, as not to make an error,
with twists spontaneously methodical.
He suddenly tasted worms windows and roses

he laughed, and closed his eyes as a girl closes
her left hand upon a mirror.

XX

my sonnet is A light goes on in
the toiletwindow, that's straightacross from
my window, night air bothered with a rustling din

sort of sublimated tom-tom
which quite outdoes the mandolin-

man's tiny racket. The horses sleep upstairs.
And you can see their ears. Ears win-

k, funny stable. In the morning they go out in pairs:
amazingly, one pair is white
(but you know that) they look at each other. Nudge.

(if they love each other, who cares?)
They pull the morning out of the night.

I am living with a mouse who shares

my meals with him, which is fair as i judge.

XXI

when you went away it was morning
(that is, big horses; light feeling up
streets; heels taking derbies (where?) a pup
hurriedly hunched over swill; one butting

trolley imposingly empty; snickering
shop doors unlocked by white-grub
faces) clothed in delicate hubbub

as you stood thinking of anything,

maybe the world . . . . But i have wondered since
isn't it odd of you really to lie
a sharp agreeable flower between my

amused legs
                    kissing with little dints

of april, making the obscene shy
breasts tickle, laughing when i wilt and wince

XXII

you asked me to come: it was raining a little,
and the spring; a clumsy brightness of air
wonderfully stumbled above the square,
little amorous-tadpole people wiggled

battered by stuttering pearl,
                                        leaves jiggled
to the jigging fragrance of newness
—and then. My crazy fingers liked your dress
. . . . your kiss, your kiss was a distinct brittle

flower, and the flesh crisp set
my love-tooth on edge. So until light
each having each we promised to forget—

wherefore is there nothing left to guess:
the cheap intelligent thighs, the electric trite
thighs; the hair stupidly priceless.

XXIII

and this day it was Spring . . . . us
drew lewdly the murmurous minute clumsy
smelloftheworld. We intricately
alive, cleaving the luminous stammer of bodies
(eagerly just not each other touch)seeking, some
street which easily trickles a brittle fuss
of fragile huge humanity . . . .
                                  Numb
thoughts, kicking in the rivers of our blood, miss
by how terrible inches speech—it
made you a little dizzy did the world's smell
(but i was thinking why the girl-and-bird
of you move . . . . moves . . . . and also, i'll admit—)

till,at the corner of Nothing and Something,we heard
a handorgan in twilight playing like hell

XXIV

i like my body when it is with your
body. It is so quite new a thing.
Muscles better and nerves more.
i like your body. i like what it does,
i like its hows. i like to feel the spine
of your body and its bones, and the trembling
-firm-smooth ness and which i will
again and again and again
kiss, i like kissing this and that of you,
i like, slowly stroking the, shocking fuzz
of your electric fur, and what-is-it comes
over parting flesh . . . . And eyes big love-crumbs,

and possibly i like the thrill

of under me you so quite new

Xli Poems

SONGS

I

the
　　sky
　　　　was
can　dy lu
minous
　　　　edible
spry
　　　pinks shy
lemons
greens　coo　l choc
olate
s.

　un　der,
　a　lo
co
mo
　　tive　s pout
　　　　　　　ing
　　　　　　vi
　　　　　　o
　　　　　　lets

II

of my
soul a street is:
prettinesses Pic-
abian tricktrickclickflick-er
garnished
of stark Picasso
throttling trees

hither
my soul
repairs herself with
prisms of sharp mind
and Matisse rhythms
to juggle Kandinsky gold-fish

away from the gripping gigantic
muscles of Cézanne's
logic,
      oho.
      a street
there is

where strange birds   purr

I I I

when life is quite through with
and leaves say alas,
much is to do
for the swallow, that closes
a flight in the blue;

when love's had his tears out,
perhaps shall pass
a million years
(while a bee dozes
on the poppies, the dears;

when all's done and said, and
under the grass
lies her head
by oaks and roses
deliberated.)

I V

into the smiting
sky   tense
with
blend

ing
the
tree   leaps
           a stiffened exquisite

i
wait the sweet
annihilation of swift
flesh

i make me stern against
your charming strength

O haste
         annihilator
drawing into you my enchanting
leaves

V

Where's Madge then,
Madge and her men?
buried with
Alice in her hair,
(but if you ask the rain
he'll not tell where.)

beauty makes terms
with time and his worms,
when loveliness
says sweetly Yes
to wind and cold;
and how much earth
is Madge worth?
Inquire of the flower that sways in the autumn
she will never guess.
but i know

VI

after five
times the poem
of thy remembrance
surprises with refrain

of unreasoning summer
that by responding
ways cloaked with renewal
my body turns toward

thee
again   for the stars have been
finished in the nobler trees and
the language of leaves repeats

eventual perfection
while east deserves of dawn.
i lie at length, breathing
with shut eyes

the sweet earth where thou liest

VII

between green
                    mountains
sings the flinger
of

fire   beyond red rivers
of fair perpetual
feet the
sinuous

riot

the
flashing
bacchant.

partedpetaled
mouth, face
delirious. indivisible
grace

    of dancing

VIII

in the rain-
darkness,   the sunset
being sheathed i sit and
think of you

the holy
city which is your face
your little cheeks the streets
of smiles

your eyes half-
thrush
half-angel and your drowsy
lips where float flowers of kiss

and
there is the sweet shy pirouette
your hair
and then

your dancesong
soul.   rarely-beloved
a single star is
uttered, and i

think
    of you

I X

Lady of Silence
from the winsome cage of
thy body
rose
    through the sensible
night
a
quick bird

(tenderly upon
the dark's prodigious face
thy
voice
    scattering perfume-gifted
wings
suddenly escorts
with feet
sun-sheer

the smarting beauty of dawn)

X

the hills
like poets put on
purple thought against
the

magnificent clamor of
                day
tortured
in gold,which presently

crumpled
collapses.
exhaling a red soul into the dark

so
duneyed master
enter
the sweet gates

                        of my heart and

take
the
rose,

which perfect
is
With killing hands

XI

i will wade out
                        till my thighs are steeped in burning flowers
I will take the sun in my mouth
and leap into the ripe air
                        Alive
                                    with closed eyes
to dash against darkness
                                    in the sleeping curves of my body
Shall enter fingers of smooth mastery
with chasteness of sea-girls
                                    Will i complete the mystery
                                    of my flesh
I will rise
            After a thousand years
lipping
flowers
            And set my teeth in the silver of the moon

XII

cruelly, love
walk the autumn long;
the last flower in whose hair,
thy lips are cold with songs

for which is
first to wither, to pass?
shallowness of sunlight
falls and, cruelly,
across the grass
Comes the
moon

love, walk the
autumn
love, for the last
flower in the hair withers;
thy hair is acold with
dreams,
love thou art frail

—walk the longness of autumn
smile dustily to the people,
for winter
who crookedly care.

CHANSONS INNOCENTES

I

why did you go
little fourpaws?
you forgot to shut
your big eyes.

where did you go?
like little kittens
are all the leaves
which open in the rain.

little kittens who
are called spring,
is what we stroke
maybe asleep?

do you know? or maybe did
something go away
ever so quietly
when we weren't looking.

II

little tree
little silent Christmas tree
you are so little
you are more like a flower

who found you in the green forest
and were you very sorry to come away?
see   i will comfort you
because you smell so sweetly

i will kiss your cool bark
and hug you safe and tight
just as your mother would,
only don't be afraid

look   the spangles
that sleep all the year in a dark box
dreaming of being taken out and allowed to shine,
the balls the chains red and gold the fluffy threads,

put up your little arms
and i'll give them all to you to hold
every finger shall have its ring
and there won't be a single place dark or unhappy

then when you're quite dressed
you'll stand in the window for everyone to see
and how they'll stare!
oh but you'll be very proud

and my little sister and i will take hands
and looking up at our beautiful tree
we'll dance and sing
"Noel Noel"

PORTRAITS

I

conversation with my friend is particularly

to enjoy the composed sudden body atop which always
quivers the electric Distinct face haughtily vital clinched
in a swoon of synopsis

despite a sadistic modesty his mind is seen frequently
fingering the exact beads of a faultless languor when
invisibly consult with some delicious image the a little
strolling lips and eyes inwardly crisping

for my friend, feeling is the sacred and agonizing
proximity to its desire of a doomed impetuous acute
sentience whose whitehot lips however suddenly ap-
proached may never quite taste the wine which their
nearness evaporates

to think is the slippery contours of a vase inexpressibly
fragile it is for the brain irrevocably frigid to touch a
merest shape which however slenderly by it caressed
will explode and spill the immediate imperceptible
content

my friend's being, out of the spontaneous clumsy trivial acrobatic edgeless gesture of existence, continually
whittles keen careful futile flowers

(isolating with perpetually meticulous concupiscence
the bright large undeniable disease of Life, himself
occasionally contrives an unreal precise intrinsic fragment of actuality),

an orchid whose velocity is sculptural

I I

one April dusk the
sallow street-lamps were turning
snowy against a west of robin's egg blue when
i entered a mad street whose

mouth dripped with slavver of
spring
chased two flights of squirrel-stairs into
a mid-victorian attic which is known as
Ο ΠΑΡΘΕΝΩΝ
                              and having ordered
yaoorti from
Nicho'
settled my feet on the

ceiling inhaling six divine inches
of Haremina   in
the thick of the snick-
er of cards and smack of back-

gammon boards i was aware of an entirely
dirty circle of habitues their
faces like cigarettebutts, chewed
with disdain,   lead by a Jumpy

Tramp who played each
card as if it were a thunderbolt red-
hot   peeling
off huge slabs of a fuzzy

language with the aid of an exclamatory
tooth-pick
And who may that
be i said exhaling into

eternity as Nicho' laid
before me bread
more downy than street-lamps
upon an almostclean

plate
"Achilles"
said
Nicho'

"and did you perhaps wish also shishkabob?"

I I I

Picasso
you give us Things
which
bulge:grunting lungs pumped full of sharp thick mind

you make us shrill
presents always
shut in the sumptuous screech of
simplicity

(out of the
black unbunged
Something gushes vaguely a squeak of planes
or

between squeals of
Nothing grabbed with circular shrieking tightness
solid screams whisper.)
Lumberman of The Distinct

your brain's
axe only chops hugest inherent
Trees of Ego,from
whose living and biggest

bodies lopped
of every
prettiness

you hew form truly

IV

the skinny voice

of the leatherfaced
woman with the crimson
nose and coquettishly-
cocked bonnet

having ceased   the

captain
announces that as three
dimes seven nickels and ten
pennies have been deposited upon

the drum   there is need

of just twenty five cents
dear friends
to make it an even
dollar   whereupon

the Divine Average who was

attracted by the inspired
sister's howling moves
off
will anyone tell him why he should

blow two bits for the coming of Christ Jesus

?
??
???
!

nix, kid

V

as usual i did not find him in cafes, the more dissolute
atmosphere of a street superimposing a numbing im-
perfectness upon such peregrinations as twilight spontaneously by inevitable tiredness of flanging shop-girls
impersonally affords furnished a soft first clue to his
innumerable whereabouts   violet logic of annihilation demonstrating from woolworthian pinacle a
capable millenium of faces meshing with my curiously
instant appreciation exposed his hibernative contours,

    aimiable immensity impeccably extending the
courtesy of five o'clock became the omen of his presence

    it was spring by the way in the soiled canary-cage
of largest existence.

(when he would extemporise the innovation of mus-
cularity upon the most crimson assistance of my com-
forter a click of deciding glory inflicted to the negative
silence that primeval exposure whose electric solidity
remembers some accurately profuse scratchings in a
recently discovered cave,   the carouse of geomet-
rical putrescence whereto my invariably commendable
room has been forever subject his Earliest word wheeled
out on the sunny dump of oblivion)

a tiny dust finely arising at the integration of my soul
i coughed

, naturally

V I

it's just like a coffin's
inside when you die,
pretentious and
shiny and
not too wide
          dear god

there's a portrait
over the door very notable of
the sultan's nose pullable and rosy
flanked by the scrumptious magdalene
of whoisit and madame
something by gainsborough

                              just the playthings
                              for dust   n'est-ce pas

   effendi drifts between
   tables like an old leaf
   between toadstools
he is the cheerfulest of men
   his peaked head smoulders
   like a new turd in April
   his legs are brittle and small
   his feet large and fragile
his queer hands twitter before him, like foolish
   butterflies
he is the most courteous of men

should you remark the walls have been repapered

he will nod
              like buddha
              or answer modestly
i am dying

so let us come in together and
drink coffee covered with froth
half-mud
and not too
sweet?

VII

my mind is
a big hunk of irrevocable nothing which touch and
taste and smell and hearing and sight keep hitting and
chipping with sharp fatal tools
in an agony of sensual chisels i perform squirms of
chrome and execute strides of cobalt
nevertheless i
feel that i cleverly am being altered that i slightly am
becoming something a little different, in fact
myself
Hereupon helpless i utter lilac shrieks and scarlet
bellowings.

VIII

5
derbies-with-men-in-them smoke Helmar
cigarettes   2
play backgammon, 3 watch

a has gold
teeth b pink
suspenders c
reads Atlantis

x and y play   b
cries "effendi" "Uh" "coffee"
"uh"   enter
paperboy, c

buys Bawstinamereekin, exit
paperboy   a finishes
Helmar   lights
another

         x and y
play, effendi approaches, sets
down coffee   withdraws
a and c discuss news in

turkish x and y play b spits
x and
y
play, b starts armenian record

                                        pho
nographisrunn
ingd o w, n   phonograph
                 stopS.

b swears in persian at phonograph
x wins   exeunt ax: by; c,
Goo dnightef fendi
. . . .

five men in derbies

I X

at the ferocious phenomenon of 5 o'clock i find myself
gently decomposing in the mouth of New York. Between its supple financial teeth deliriously sprouting
from complacent gums, a morsel prettily wanders
buoyed on the murderous saliva of industry. the morsel is i.

Vast cheeks enclose me.

a gigantic uvula with imperceptible gesticulations
threatens the tubular downward blackness occasionally
from which detatching itself bumps clumsily into the
throat A meticulous vulgarity:

a sodden fastidious normal explosion; a square murmur, a winsome flatulence—

In the soft midst of the tongue sits the Woolworth
building a serene pastile-shaped insipid kinesis or frail
swooping lozenge. a ruglike sentience whose papillæ
expertly drink the docile perpendicular taste of this
squirming cube of undiminished silence, supports
while devouring the firm tumult of exquisitely in-
secure sharp algebraic music. For the first time in

sorting from this vast nonchalant inward walk of volume the flat minute gallop of careful hugeness i am
conjugated by the sensual mysticism of entire vertical
being, i am skilfully construed by a delicately experi-
menting colossus whose irrefutable spiral antics involve
me with the soothings of plastic hypnotism   . i am
accurately parsed by this gorgeous rush of upward
lips. . . .

cleverly

perching on the sudden extremity of one immense
tooth myself surveys safely the complete important
profane frantic inconsequential gastronomic mystery
of mysteries
                , life.

Far below myself the lunging leer of horizontal large
distinct ecstasy wags and. rages Laughters jostle grins
nudge smiles push—.deep into the edgeless gloaming
gladness hammers incessant putrid spikes of madness
(at

Myself's height these various innocent ferocities are
superceded by the sole prostituted ferocity of silence,
it is) still 5 o'clock
I stare only always into the tremendous canyon the

, tremendous canyon always only exhales a climbing
dark exact walloping human noise of digestible millions whose rich slovenly obscene procession always
floats through the thin amorous enormous only lips of
the evening

    And it is 5 o'clock

    in the oblong air, from which a singular ribbon
of common sunset is hanging,

snow speaks slowly

LA GUERRE

I

earth like a tipsy
biddy with an old mop punching
underneath
conventions exposes

hidden obscenities
nudging
into neglected sentiments brings
to light dusty

heroisms
and
finally colliding with the most
expensive furniture upsets

a
crucifix which smashes into several
pieces and is hurriedly picked up and
thrown on the ash-heap

where
lies
        what was once the discobolus of
one

Myron

II

Humanity i love you
because you would rather black the boots of
success than enquire whose soul dangles from his
watch-chain which would be embarrassing for both

parties and because you
unflinchingly applaud all
songs containing the words country home and
mother when sung at the old howard

Humanity i love you because
when you're hard up you pawn your
intelligence to buy a drink and when
you're flush pride keeps

you from the pawn shop and
because you are continually committing
nuisances but more
especially in your own house

Humanity i love you because you
are perpetually putting the secret of
life in your pants and forgetting
it's there and sitting down

on it
and because you are
forever making poems in the lap
of death Humanity

i hate you

SONNETS

I

if learned darkness from our searched world

should wrest the rare unwisdom of thy eyes,
and if thy hands flowers of silence curled

upon a wish, to rapture should surprise
my soul slowly which on thy beauty dreams
(proud through the cold perfect night whisperless

to mark, how that asleep whitely she seems

whose lips the whole of life almost do guess)

if god should send the morning; and before
my doubting window leaves softly to stir,
of thoughtful trees whom night hath pondered o'er
—and frailties of dimension to occur

about us
                    and birds known, scarcely to sing

(heart, could we bear the marvel of this thing?)

II

O Thou to whom the musical white spring

offers her lily inextinguishable,
taught by thy tremulous grace bravely to fling

Implacable death's mysteriously sable
robe from her redolent shoulders,
                                    Thou from whose
feet reincarnate song suddenly leaping
flameflung, mounts, inimitably to lose
herself where the wet stars softly are keeping

their exquisite dreams—O Love! upon thy dim
shrine of intangible commemoration,
(from whose faint close as some grave languorous hymn

pledged to illimitable dissipation
unhurried clouds of incense fleetly roll)

i spill my bright incalculable soul.

III

when unto nights of autumn do complain
earth's ghastlier trees by whom Time measured is
when frost to dance maketh the sagest pane
of littler huts with peerless fantasies
or the unlovely longness of the year

droops with things dead athwart the narrowing hours
and hope (by cold espoused unto fear)
in dreadful corners hideously cowers—

i do excuse me, love, to Death and Time

storms and rough cold, wind's menace and leaf's grieving:
from the impressed fingers of sublime
Memory, of that loveliness receiving
the image my proud heart cherished as fair.

(The child-head poised with the serious hair)

I V

this is the garden: colours come and go,
frail azures fluttering from night's outer wing
strong silent greens serenely lingering,
absolute lights like baths of golden snow.
This is the garden: pursed lips do blow
upon cool flutes within wide glooms, and sing
(of harps celestial to the quivering string)
invisible faces hauntingly and slow.

This is the garden. Time shall surely reap
and on Death's blade lie many a flower curled,
in other lands where other songs be sung;
yet stand They here enraptured, as among
the slow deep trees perpetual of sleep
some silver-fingered fountain steals the world.

V

Thou in whose swordgreat story shine the deeds
of history her heroes, sounds the tread
of those vast armies of the marching dead,
with standards and the neighing of great steeds
moving to war across the smiling meads;
thou by whose page we break the precious bread
of dear communion with the past, and wed
to valor, battle with heroic breeds;

thou, Froissart, for that thou didst love the pen
while others wrote in steel, accept all praise
of after ages, and of hungering days
for whom the old glories move, the old trumpets cry;
who gavest as one of those immortal men
his life that his fair city might not die.

VI

when the proficient poison of sure sleep
bereaves us of our slow tranquillities

and He without Whose favour nothing is
(being of men called Love) upward doth leap
from the mute hugeness of depriving deep,

with thunder of those hungering wings of His,

into the lucent and large signories
—i shall not smile beloved; i shall not weep:

when from the less-than-whiteness of thy face
(whose eyes inherit vacancy) will time
extract his inconsiderable doom,
when these thy lips beautifully embrace
nothing
            and when thy bashful hands assume

silence beyond the mystery of rhyme

VII

and what were roses.   Perfume? for i do
forget . . . . or mere Music mounting unsurely

twilight
            but here were something more maturely
childish, more beautiful almost than you.

Yet if not flower, tell me softly who

be these haunters of dreams always demurely
halfsmiling from cool faces, moving purely
with muted step, yet somewhat proudly too—

are they not ladies, ladies of my dreams
justly touching roses their fingers whitely
live by?
            or better,
                        queens, queens laughing lightly
crowned with far colours,

                          thinking very much
of nothing and whom dawn loves most to touch

wishing by willows, bending upon streams?

VIII

come nothing to my comparable soul
which with existence has conversed in vain,
O scrupulously take thy trivial toll,
for whose cool feet this frantic heart is fain;
try me with thy perfumes which have seduced
the mightier nostrils of the fervent dead,
feed with felicities me wormperused
by whom the hungering mouth of time is fed:
and if i like not what thou givest me
to him let me complain, whose seat is where
revolving planets struggle to be free
with the astounding everlasting air—
but if i like, i'll take between thy hands
what no man feels, no woman understands.

IX

when my sensational moments are no more
unjoyously bullied of vilest mind

and sweet uncaring earth by thoughtful war
heaped wholly with high wilt of human rind—
when over hate has triumphed darkly love

and the small spiritual cry of spring
utters a striving flower,
                          just where strove
the droll god-beasts

                    do thou distinctly bring
thy footstep, and the rushing of thy deep
hair and the smiting smile didst love to use
in other days (drawing my Mes from sleep
whose stranger dreams thy strangeness must abuse . . . .)

Time being not for us, purple roses were
sweeter to thee
                    perchance to me deeper.

X

I have seen her a stealthily frail
flower walking with its fellows in the death
of light, against whose enormous curve of flesh
exactly cubes of tiny fragrance try;
i have watched certain petals rapidly wish
in the corners of her youth; whom, fiercely shy
and gently brutal, the prettiest wrath
of blossoms dishevelling made a pale
fracas upon the accurate moon . . . .
Across the important gardens her body
will come toward me with its hurting sexual smell
of lilies . . . . beyond night's silken immense swoon
the moon is like a floating silver hell
a song of adolescent ivory.

X I

who's most afraid of death? thou
                              art of him
utterly afraid, i love of thee
(beloved) this

            and truly i would be
near when his scythe takes crisply the whim
of thy smoothness. and mark the fainting
murdered petals. with the caving stem.

But of all most would i be one of them

round the hurt heart which do so frailly cling . . . .)
i who am but imperfect in my fear

Or with thy mind against my mind, to hear
nearing our hearts' irrevocable play—
through the mysterious high futile day

an enormous stride
                  (and drawing thy mouth toward

my mouth, steer our lost bodies carefully downward)

XII

perhaps it is to feel strike
the silver fish of her nakedness
with fins sharply pleasant, my

youth has travelled toward her these years

or to snare the timid like
of her mind to my mind that i

am come by little countries to the yes

of her youth.
        And if somebody hears
what i say—let him be pitiful:
because i've travelled all alone
through the forest of wonderful,
and that my feet have surely known
the furious ways and the peaceful,

and because she is beautiful

XIII

when i am in Boston, i do not speak.
and i sit in the click of ivory balls . . . .

noting flies, which jerk upon the weak
colour of table-cloths, the electric When
In Doubt Buy Of (but a roof hugs
whom)
        as the august evening mauls
Kneeland, and a waiter cleverly lugs
indigestible honeycake to men
. . . . one perfectly smooth coffee
tasting of hellas, i drink, or sometimes two
remarking cries of paklavah meeah.
(Very occasionally three.)
and i gaze on the cindercoloured little ΜΕΓΑ
ΕΛΛΗΝΙΚΟΝ ΞΕΝΟΔΟΧΕΙΟΝ ΥΠΝΟΥ

XIV

will suddenly trees leap from winter and will

the stabbing music of your white youth
wounded by my arms' bothness
(say a twilight lifting the fragile skill
of new leaves' voices, and sharp lips of spring
simply joining with the wonderless
city's sublime cheap distinct mouth)

do the exact human comely thing?

(or will the fleshless moments go and go

across this dirtied pane where softly preys
the grey and perpendicular Always—
or possibly there drift a pulseless blur
of paleness;
         the unswift mouths of snow
insignificantly whisper. . . .

XV

a fragrant sag of fruit distinctly grouped.

I have not eaten peppers for a week.

On this street the houses immensely speak
(it is nine minutes past six)

the well-fed L's immaculate roar looped
straightens, into neatest distance. . . .

A new curve of children gladly cricks
where a hurdy-gurdy accurately pants.

and pompous ancient jews obscurely twitch
through the bumping teem of Grand. a nudging froth
of faces clogs Second as Mrs. Somethingwich

(with flesh like an old toy baloon)

heavily swims to Strunsky's,

         Monia's mouth
eats tangerines looking at the moon—

XVI

by god i want above fourteenth

fifth's deep purring biceps, the mystic screech
of Broadway, the trivial stink of rich

frail firm asinine life
      (i pant

for what's below. the singer. Wall. i want
the perpendicular lips the insane teeth
the vertical grin

       give me the Square in spring,
the little barbarous Greenwich perfumed fake

And most, the futile fooling labyrinth
where noisy colors stroll . . . . and the Baboon

sniggering insipidities while. i sit, sipping
singular anisettes as. One opaque
big girl jiggles thickly hips to the canoun

but Hassan chuckles seeing the Greeks breathe)

IS 5

FOREWORD

On the assumption that my technique is either complicated or original or both, the publishers have politely requested me to write an introduction to this book.

At least my theory of technique, if I have one, is very far from original; nor is it complicated. I can express it in fifteen words, by quoting The Eternal Question And Immortal Answer of burlesk, viz. "Would you hit a woman with a child?—No, I'd hit her with a brick." Like the burlesk comedian, I am abnormally fond of that precision which creates movement.

If a poet is anybody, he is somebody to whom things made matter very little—somebody who is obsessed by Making. Like all obsessions, the Making obsession has disadvantages; for instance, my only interest in making money would be to make it. Fortunately, however, I should prefer to make almost anything else, including locomotives and roses. It is with roses and locomotives (not to mention acrobats Spring electricity Coney Island the 4th of July the eyes of mice and Niagara Falls) that my "poems" are competing.

They are also competing with each other, with elephants, and with El Greco.

Ineluctable preoccupation with The Verb gives a poet one priceless advantage: whereas nonmakers must content themselves with the merely undeniable fact that two times two is four, he rejoices in a purely irresistible truth (to be found, in abbreviated costume, upon the title page of the present volume).

E. E. CUMMINGS.

One

I

FIVE AMERICANS

I. LIZ

with breathing as (faithfully) her lownecked
dress a little topples and slightly expands

one square foot mired in silk wrinkling loth
stocking begins queerly to do a few
gestures to death,
                    the silent shoulders are both
slowly with pinkish ponderous arms bedecked
whose white thick wrists deliver promptly to
a deep lap enormous mindless hands.
and no one knows what (i am sure of this)
her blunt unslender, what her big unkeen

"Business is rotten" the face yawning said

what her mouth thinks of
                            (if it were a kiss
distinct entirely melting sinuous lean . . .
whereof this lady in some book had read

II. MAME

she puts down the handmirror. "Look at" arranging
before me a mellifluous idiot grin
(with what was nose upwrinkled into nothing
earthly, while the slippery eyes drown
in surging flesh). A thumblike index down-
dragging yanks back skin "see" (i, seeing, ceased
to breathe). The plump left fist opening
"wisdom." Flicker of gold. "Yep. No gas. Flynn"

the words drizzle untidily from released
cheeks "I'll tell duh woild; some noive all right.
Aint much on looks but how dat baby ached."

and when i timidly hinted "novocaine?"
the eyes outstart, curl, bloat, are newly baked

and swaggering cookies of indignant light

III. GERT

joggle i think will do it although the glad
monosyllable jounce possibly can tell
better how the balloons move (as
her ghost lurks, a Beau Brummel sticking in its three-

cornered always moist mouth)—jazz,
for whose twitching lips, between you and me
almost succeeds while toddle rings the bell.
But if her tall corpsecoloured body seat
itself (with the uncouth habitual dull
jerk at garters) there 's no sharpest neat
word for the thing.
             Her voice?

                      gruesome: a trull
leaps from the lungs "gimme uh swell fite

like up ter yknow, Rektuz, Toysday nite;
where uh guy gets gayn troze uh lobstersalad

IV. MARJ

"life?
        Listen" the feline she with radishred
legs said (crossing them slowly) "I'm
asleep. Yep. Youse is asleep kid
and everybody is." And i hazarded
"god" (blushing slightly)—"O damn
ginks like dis Gawd" opening slowlyslowly
them—then carefully the rolypoly
voice squatting on a mountain of gum did
something like a whisper, "even her."
"The Madam?" I emitted; vaguely watching
that mountainous worthy in the fragile act
of doing her eyebrows.—Marj's laughter smacked
me: pummeling the curtains, drooped to a purr . . .

i left her permanently smiling

should i entirely ask of god why
on the alert neck of this brittle whore
delicately wobbles an improbably distinct face,
and how these wooden big two feet conclude
happeningly the unfirm drooping bloated
calves
          i would receive the answer more
or less deserved, Young fellow go in peace.
which i do, being as Dick Mid once noted
lifting a Green River (here's to youse)
"a bloke wot's well behaved" . . . and always try
to not wonder how let's say elation
causes the bent eyes thickly to protrude—

or why her tiniest whispered invitation
is like a clock striking in a dark house

II
POEM, OR BEAUTY HURTS MR. VINAL

take it from me kiddo
believe me
my country, 'tis of

you, land of the Cluett
Shirt Boston Garter and Spearmint
Girl With The Wrigley Eyes (of you
land of the Arrow Ide
and Earl &
Wilson
Collars) of you i
sing:land of Abraham Lincoln and Lydia E. Pinkham,
land above all of Just Add Hot Water And Serve—
from every B. V. D.

let freedom ring

amen. i do however protest, anent the un
-spontaneous and otherwise scented merde which
greets one (Everywhere Why) as divine poesy per
that and this radically defunct periodical. i would

suggest that certain ideas gestures
rhymes, like Gillette Razor Blades
having been used and reused
to the mystical moment of dullness emphatically **are**
Not To Be Resharpened.   (Case in point

if we are to believe these gently O sweetly
melancholy trillers amid the thrillers
these crepuscular violinists among my and your
skyscrapers— Helen & Cleopatra were Just Too Lovely,
The Snail's On The Thorn enter Morn and God's
In His andsoforth

do you get me?) according
to such supposedly indigenous
throstles Art is O World O Life
a formula: example, Turn Your Shirttails Into
Drawers and If It Isn't An Eastman It Isn't A
Kodak therefore my friends let
us now sing each and all fortissimo A-
mer
i

ca, I
love,
You.   And there're a
hun-dred-mil-lion-oth-ers, like
all of you successfully if
delicately gelded (or spaded)
gentlemen (and ladies)— pretty

littleliverpill-
hearted-Nujolneeding-There's-A-Reason
americans (who tensetendoned and with
upward vacant eyes, painfully
perpetually crouched, quivering, upon the
sternly allotted sandpile
—how silently
emit a tiny violetflavoured nuisance: Odor?

ono.
comes out like a ribbon lies flat on the brush

III

curtains part)
the peacockappareled
prodigy of Flo's midnight
Frolic dolores

small in the head keen chassised like a Rolls
Royce
swoops smoothly
                    outward(amid
tinkling-cheering-hammering

tables)

while softly along Kirkland Street
the infantile ghost of Professor
Royce rolls

remembering that it

has for
-gotten some-
thing ah

(my

necktie

IV

workingman with hand so hairy-sturdy
you may turn O turn that airy hurdysturdygurdy
but when will turn backward O backward Time in your no thy flight
and make me a child, a pretty dribbling child, a little child.

In thy your ear:
en amérique on ne boit que de Jingyale.
things are going rather kaka
over there, over there.
yet we scarcely fare much better—

what's become of (if you please)
all the glory that or which was Greece
all the grandja
that was dada?

make me a child, stout hurdysturdygurdyman
waiter, make me a child. So this is Paris.
i will sit in the corner and drink thinks and think drinks,
in memory of the Grand and Old days:
of Amy Sandburg
of Algernon Carl Swinburned.

Waiter a drink waiter two or three drinks
what's become of Maeterlinck
now that April's here?
(ask the man who owns one
ask Dad, He knows).

V

    yonder deadfromtheneckup graduate of a
    somewhat obscure to be sure university spends
    her time looking picturesque under

    the as it happens quite
    erroneous impression that he

    nascitur

VI

    Jimmie's got a goil
              goil
                   goil,
                        Jimmie
    's got a goil and
    she coitnly can shimmie

    when you see her shake
              shake
                   shake,
                        when
    you see her shake a
    shimmie how you wish that you was Jimmie.

Oh for such a gurl
                gurl
                    gurl,
                          oh
for such a gurl to
be a fellow's twistandtwirl

talk about your Sal-
                Sal-
                    Sal-,
                        talk
about your Salo
-mes but gimmie Jimmie's gal.

VII

listen my children and you
shall hear the true

story of **Mr Do**
-nothing the wellknown parvenu
who

(having dreamed of a corkscrew)
studied with Freud a year or two
and when Freud got through
with Do-

nothing Do
-nothing could do
nothing which you
and i are accustomed to
accomplish two

or three times, and even a few
more depending on the remu-
nerativeness of the stimulus(eheu
fu
-gaces Postu-
me boo

who)

VIII

even if all desires things moments be
murdered known photographed,ourselves yawning will ask ourselves
où sont les neiges. . . . some

guys talks big

about Lundun Burlin an gay Paree an
some guys claims der never was
nutn like Nooer Leans Shikahgo Sain
Looey Noo York an San Fran dictaphones
wireless subways vacuum
cleaners pianolas funnygraphs skyscrapers an safetyrazors

sall right in its way kiddo
but as fer i gimme de good ole daze. . . .

in dem daze kid Christmas
meant sumpn youse knows wot
i refers ter Satter Nailyuh(comes but once er
year)i'll tell de woild one swell bangup
time wen nobody wore no cloze
an went runnin aroun wid eachudder Hell
Bent fer election makin believe dey was chust born

IX

death is more than
certain a hundred these
sounds crowds odours it
is in a hurry
beyond that any this
taxi smile or angle we do

not sell and buy
things so necessary as
is death and unlike shirts
neckties trousers
we cannot wear it out

            no sir which is why
            granted who discovered
            America ether the movies
            may claim general importance

            to me to you nothing is
            what particularly
            matters hence in a

            little sunlight and less
            moonlight ourselves against the worms

            hate laugh shimmy

                          X

nobody loses all the time

i had an uncle named
Sol who was a born failure and
nearly everybody said he should have gone
into vaudeville perhaps because my Uncle Sol could
sing McCann He Was A Diver on Xmas Eve like Hell Itself which
may or may not account for the fact that my Uncle

Sol indulged in that possibly most inexcusable
of all to use a highfalootin phrase
luxuries that is or to
wit farming and be
it needlessly
added

my Uncle Sol's farm
failed because the chickens
ate the vegetables so
my Uncle Sol had a
chicken farm till the
skunks ate the chickens when

my Uncle Sol
had a skunk farm but
the skunks caught cold and
died and so
my Uncle Sol imitated the
skunks in a subtle manner

or by drowning himself in the watertank
but somebody who'd given my Uncle Sol a Victor
Victrola and records while he lived presented to
him upon the auspicious occasion of his decease a
scrumptious not to mention splendiferous funeral with
tall boys in black gloves and flowers and everything and

i remember we all cried like the Missouri
when my Uncle Sol's coffin lurched because
somebody pressed a button
(and down went
my Uncle
Sol

and started a worm farm)

XI

now dis "daughter" uv eve(who aint precisely slim)sim

ply don't know duh meanin uv duh woid sin in
not disagreeable contras tuh dat not exacly fat

"father"(adjustin his robe)who now puts on his flat hat

XII

(and i imagine
never mind Joe agreeably cheerfully remarked when
surrounded by fat stupid animals
the jewess shrieked
the messiah tumbled successfully into the world
the animals continued eating. And i imagine she, and
heard them slobber and
in the darkness)

stood sharp angels with faces like Jim Europe

XIII

it really must
be Nice, never to

have no imagination)or never
never to wonder about guys you used to(and them
slim hot queens with dam next to nothing

on)tangoing
(while a feller tries
to hold down the fifty bucks per
job with one foot and rock a

cradle with the other)it Must be
nice never to have no doubts about why you
put the ring
on(and watching her
face grow old and tired to which

you're married and hands get red washing
things and dishes)and to never, never really wonder i
mean about the smell
of babies and how you

know the dam rent's going to and everything and never, never
Never to stand at no window
because i can't sleep(smoking sawdust

cigarettes in the
middle of the night

XIV
ITEM

this man is o so
Waiter
this;woman is

please shut that
the pout And affectionate leer
interminable pyramidal,napkins
(this man is oh so tired of this
a door opens by itself
woman.) they so to speak were in

Love once?
now
　　　　her mouth opens too far
and:she attacks her Lobster without
feet mingle under the
mercy.
　　　　(exit the hors d'œuvres)

X V

IKEY(GOLDBERG)'S WORTH I'M
TOLD $ SEVERAL MILLION
FINKLESTEIN(FRITZ)LIVES
AT THE RITZ WEAR
earl & wilson COLLARS

X V I
?

why are these pipples taking their hets off?
the king & queen
alighting from their limousine
inhabit the Hôtel Meurice(whereas
i live in a garret and eat aspirine)

but who is this pale softish almost round
young man to whom headwaiters bow so?
hush—the author of Women By Night whose latest Seeds
Of Evil sold 69 carloads before
publication the girl who goes wrong you

know(whereas when i lie down i cough too
much). How did the traffic get so jammed?
bedad it is the famous doctor who inserts
monkeyglands in millionaires a cute idea n'est-ce pas?
(whereas, upon the other hand, myself)but let us next demand

wherefore yon mob
an accident? somebody got concus-
sion of the brain?—Not
a bit of it, my dears merely the prime
minister of Siam in native

costume, who
emerging from a pissoir
enters abruptly Notre Dame(whereas
de gustibus non disputandum est
my lady is tired of That sort of thing

XVII

this young question mark man

question mark
who suffers from
indigestion question
mark is a remarkably
charming person

personally they tell

me as for me
i only knows that
as far as
his picture goes

he's a wet dream

by Cézanne

XVIII

mr youse needn't be so spry
concernin questions arty

each has his tastes but as for i
i likes a certain party

gimme the he-man's solid bliss
for youse ideas i'll match youse

a pretty girl who naked is
is worth a million statues

XIX

she being Brand

-new;and you
know consequently a
little stiff i was
careful of her and(having

thoroughly oiled the universal
joint tested my gas felt of
her radiator made sure her springs were O.

K.)i went right to it flooded-the-carburetor cranked her

up,slipped the
clutch(and then somehow got into reverse she
kicked what
the hell)next
minute i was back in neutral tried and

again slo-wly;bare,ly nudg.   ing(my

lev-er Right-
oh and her gears being in
A 1 shape passed
from low through
second-in-to-high like
greasedlightning)just as we turned the corner of Divinity

avenue i touched the accelerator and give

her the juice,good

                    (it
was the first ride and believe i we was
happy to see how nice she acted right up to
the last minute coming back down by the Public
Gardens i slammed on
the

internalexpanding
&
externalcontracting
brakes Bothatonce and

brought allofher tremB
-ling
to a:dead.

stand-
;Still)

XX

slightly before the middle of Congressman Pudd
's 4th of July oration, with a curse and a frown
Amy Lowell got up
and all the little schoolchildren sat down

XXI
oDE

o

the sweet *&* aged people
who rule this world(and me **and**
you if we're **not very**
careful)

O,

the darling benevolent mindless
He—and She—
shaped waxworks filled
with dead ideas(the oh

quintillions of incredible
dodderingly godly toothless
always-so-much-interested-
in-everybody-else's-business

bipeds)OH
the bothering
dear unnecessary hairless
o

ld

XXII

on the Madam's best april the
twenty nellie

anyway and
it's flutters everything
queer;does smells he smiles is
like Out of doors he's a with
eyes and making twice the a week
you kind of,know(kind well of
A sort of the way he smile)but
and her a I mean me a
Irish,cook but well oh don't
you makes burst want to dear somehow
quickyes when(now,dark dear oh)
the iceman
how,luminously
oh how listens and,expands
my somewherealloverme heart my
the halfgloom coolish
of The what are
parks for wiggle yes has
are leap,which,anyway

give rapid lapfulls of
idiotic big hands

XXIII

(as that named Fred
-someBody:hippopotamus, scratch-
ing,one,knee with,its,
friend observes I

pass Mr Tom Larsen twirls among

paſe lips the extinct
cigar)at

which

this(once flinger
of lariats lean exroper of
horned suddenly crashing things)man spits

quickly into the very bright spittoon

XXIV

my uncle
Daniel fought in the civil
war band and can play the triangle
like the devil)my

uncle Frank has done nothing for many
years but fly kites and
when the
string breaks(or something)my uncle Frank breaks into
tears. my uncle Tom

knits and is a kewpie above the ears(but

my uncle Ed
that's
dead from the neck

up is lead all over
Brattle Street by a castrated pup

XXV

than(by yon sunset's wintry glow
revealed)this tall strong stalwart youth,
what sight shall human optics know
more quite ennobling forsooth?

One wondrous fine sonofabitch
(to all purposes and intents)
in which distinct and rich
portrait should be included,gents

these(by the fire's ruddy glow
united)not less than sixteen
children and of course you know
their mother,of his heart the queen

—incalculable bliss!
Picture it gents:our hero,Dan
who as you've guessed already is
the poorbuthonest workingman

(by that bright flame whose myriad tints
enrich a visage simple,terse,
seated like any king or prince
upon his uncorrupted arse

with all his hearty soul aglow)
his nightly supper sups
it isn't snowing snow you know
it's snowing buttercups

XXVI

weazened Irrefutable unastonished
two,countenances seated in arranging;sunlight
with-ered unspea-king:tWeNtY,f i n g e r s,large
four gnarled lips totter

Therefore,approaching my twentysix selves
bulging in immortal Spring express a cry of
How do you find the sun,ladies?

(graduallyverygradually"there is not enough
of it"their,hands
minutely

answered

XXVII
MEMORABILIA

stop look &

listen Venezia: incline thine
ear you glassworks
of Murano;
pause
elevator nel
mezzo del cammin' that means half-
way up the Campanile, believe

thou me cocodrillo—

mine eyes have seen
the glory of

the coming of
the Americans particularly the
brand of marriageable nymph which is
armed with large legs rancid
voices Baedekers Mothers and kodaks
—by night upon the Riva Schiavoni or in
the felicitous vicinity of the de l'Europe

Grand and Royal
Danielli their numbers

are like unto the stars of Heaven. . . .

i do signore
affirm that all gondola signore
day below me gondola signore gondola
and above me pass loudly and gondola
rapidly denizens of Omaha Altoona or what
not enthusiastic cohorts from Duluth God only,
gondola knows Cincingondolanati i gondola don't

—the substantial dollarbringing virgins

"from the Loggia where
are we angels by O yes
beautiful we now pass through the look
girls in the style of that's the
foliage what is it didn't Ruskin
says about you got the haven't Marjorie
isn't this wellcurb simply darling"
      —O Education:O

thos cook & son

(O to be a metope
now that triglyph's here)

XXVIII

  a man who had fallen among thieves
  lay by the roadside on his back
  dressed in fifteenthrate ideas
  wearing a round jeer for a hat

  fate per a somewhat more than less
  emancipated evening
  had in return for consciousness
  endowed him with a changeless grin

  whereon a dozen staunch and leal
  citizens did graze at pause
  then fired by hypercivic zeal
  sought newer pastures or because

  swaddled with a frozen brook
  of pinkest vomit out of eyes
  which noticed nobody he looked
  as if he did not care to rise

  one hand did nothing on the vest
  its wideflung friend clenched weakly dirt
  while the mute trouserfly confessed
  a button solemnly inert.

  Brushing from whom the stiffened puke
  i put him all into my arms
  and staggered banged with terror through
  a million billion trillion stars

XXIX

this evangelist
buttons with his big gollywog voice
the kingdomofheaven up behind and crazily
skating thither and hither in filthy sawdust
chucks and rolls
against the tent his thick joggling fists

he is persuasive

the editor cigarstinking hobgoblin swims
upward in his swivelchair one fist dangling scandal while
five other fingers snitch
rapidly through mist a defunct king as

linotypes gobblehobble

our lightheavy twic twoc ingly attacks
landing a onetwo
which doubles up suddenly his bunged hinging
victim against the
giving ropes amid
screams of deeply bulging thousands

i too omit one kelly

in response to howjedooze the candidate's new silk
lid bounds gently from his baldness
a smile masturbates softly in the vacant
lot of his physiognomy
his scientifically pressed trousers ejaculate spats

a strikingly succulent getup

but
we knew a muffhunter and he said to us Kid.
daze nutn like it.

XXX

(ponder,darling,these busted statues
of yon motheaten forum be aware
notice what hath remained
—the stone cringes
clinging to the stone,how obsolete

lips utter their extant smile . . . .
remark

a few deleted of texture
or meaning monuments and dolls

resist Them Greediest Paws of careful
time all of which is extremely
unimportant)whereas Life

matters if or

when the your- and my-
idle vertical worthless
self unite in a peculiarly
momentary

partnership(to instigate
constructive
            Horizontal
business . . . . even so,let us make haste
—consider well this ruined aqueduct

lady,
which used to lead something into somewhere)

XXXI

poets yeggs and thirsties

since we are spanked and put to sleep by dolls let
us not be continually astonished should
from their actions and speeches
sawdust perpetually leak

rather is it between such beddings and
bumpings of ourselves to be observed
how in this fundamental respect the well
recognised regime of childhood is reversed

meantime in dreams let us investigate
thoroughly each one his optima rerum first
having taken care to lie upon our
abdomens for greater privacy and lest

punished bottoms interrupt philosophy

XXXII

Will i ever forget that precarious moment?

As i was standing on the third rail waiting for the
next train to grind me into lifeless atoms various absurd thoughts slyly crept into my highly sexed mind.

It seemed to me that i had first of all really made
quite a mistake in being at all born, seeing that i was
wifeless and only half awake, cursed with pimples,
correctly dressed, cleanshaven above the nombril, and
much to my astonishment much impressed by having
once noticed (as an infantile phenomenon) George
Washington almost incompletely surrounded by well-
drawn icecakes beheld being too strong, in brief : an
American, if you understand that i mean what i say i
believe my most intimate friends would never have
gathered.

A collarbutton which had always not nothurt me not
much and in the same place.

Why according to tomorrow's paper the proletariat
will not rise yesterday.

Inexpressible itchings to be photographed with Lord
Rothermere playing with Lord Rothermere billiards
very well by moonlight with Lord Rothermere.

A crocodile eats a native, who in revenge beats it insensible with a banana, establishing meanwhile a religious cult based on consubstantial intangibility.

Personne ne m'aime et j'ai les mains froides.

His Royal Highness said "peek-a-boo" and thirty tame fleas left the prettily embroidered howdah immediately.

Thumbprints of an angel named Frederick found on a lightning-rod, Boston, Mass.

such were the not unhurried reflections to which my organ of imperception gave birth to which i should ordinarily have objected to which, considering the background, it is hardly surprising if anyone hardly should call exactly extraordinary. We refer, of course, to my position. A bachelor incapable of occupation, he had long suppressed the desire to suppress the suppressed desire of shall we say: Idleness, while meaning its opposite? Nothing could be clearer to all concerned than that i am not a policeman.

Meanwhile the tea regressed.

Kipling again H. G. Wells, and Anatole France shook hands again and yet again shook again hands again, the former coachman with a pipewrench of the again latter then opening a box of newly without exaggeration shot with some difficulty sardines. Mr. Wiggin took Wrs. Miggin's harm in is, extinguishing the spittoon by a candle furnished by courtesy of the management on Thursdays, opposite which a church stood perfectly upright but not piano item: a watermelon causes indigestion to William Cullen Longfellow's small negro son, Henry Wadsworth Bryant.

By this time, however, the flight of crows had ceased. I withdrew my hands from the tennisracket. All was over. One brief convulsive octopus, and then our hero folded his umbrella.

It seemed too beautiful.

Let us perhaps excuse me if i repeat himself: these, or nearly these, were the not unpainful thoughts which occupied the subject of our attention;to speak even less objectively, i was horribly scared i would actually fall off the rail before the really train after all arrived. If i should have made this perfectly clear, it entirely would have been not my fault.

XXXIII

voices to voices, lip to lip
i swear (to noone everyone) constitutes
undying; or whatever this and that petal confutes . . .
to exist being a peculiar form of sleep

what's beyond logic happens beneath will;
nor can these moments be translated: i say
that even after April
by God there is no excuse for May

—bring forth your flowers and machinery: sculpture and prose
flowers guess and miss
machinery is the more accurate, yes
it delivers the goods, Heaven knows

(yet are we mindful, though not as yet awake,
of ourselves which shout and cling, being
for a little while and which easily break
in spite of the best overseeing)

i mean that the blond absence of any program
except last and always and first to live
makes unimportant what i and you believe;
not for philosophy does this rose give a damn . . .

bring on your fireworks, which are a mixed
splendor of piston and of pistil; very well
provided an instant may be fixed
so that it will not rub, like any other pastel.

(While you and i have lips and voices which
are for kissing and to sing with
who cares if some oneeyed son of a bitch
invents an instrument to measure Spring with?

each dream nascitur, is not made . . .)
why then to Hell with that: the other; this,
since the thing perhaps is
to eat flowers and not to be afraid.

XXXIV

life hurl my
yes,crumbles hand(ful released conarefetti)ev eryflitter,inga. where
mil(lions of aflickf)litter ing brightmillion ofS hurl;edindodg:ing
whom areEyes shy-dodge is bright cruMbshandful,quick-hurl edinwho
Is flittercrumbs,fluttercrimbs are floatfallin,g;allwhere:
a:crimbflitteringish is arefloatsis ingfallall!mil,shy milbrightlions
my(hurl flicker handful
in)dodging are shybrigHteyes is crum bs(alll)if,ey Es

Two

I

the season 'tis, my lovely lambs,

of Sumner Volstead Christ and Co.
the epoch of Mann's righteousness
the age of dollars and no sense.
Which being quite beyond dispute

as prove from Troy (N. Y.) to Cairo
(Egypt) the luminous dithyrambs
of large immaculate unmute
antibolshevistic gents
(each manufacturing word by word
his own unrivalled brand of pyro
-technic blurb anent the (hic)
hero dead that gladly (sic)
in far lands perished of unheard
of maladies including flu)

my little darlings, let us now
passionately remember how—
braving the worst, of peril heedless,
each braver than the other, each
(a typewriter within his reach)
upon his fearless derrière
sturdily seated—Colonel Needless
To Name and General You know who
a string of pretty medals drew

(while messrs jack james john and jim
in token of their country's love
received my dears the order of
The Artificial Arm and Limb)

—or, since bloodshed and kindred questions
inhibit unprepared digestions,
come: let us mildly contemplate
beginning with his wellfilled pants
earth's biggest grafter, nothing less;
the Honorable Mr. (guess)
who, breathing on the ear of fate,
landed a seat in the legislat-
ure whereas tommy so and so
(an erring child of circumstance
whom the bulls nabbed at 33rd)

pulled six months for selling snow

I I

opening of the chambers close

quotes the microscopic pithicoid President
in a new frock
coat(scrambling all
up over the tribune dances crazily
&&)&
chatters about Peacepeacepeace(to
droppingly
descend amid thunderous anthropoid applause)pronounced

by the way Pay the

extremely artistic nevertobeextinguished fla
-me of the(very prettily indeed)arra-
nged souvenir of the in spite of himself fa
-mous soldier minus his na-
me(so as not to hurt the perspective of the(hei
-nous thought)otherwise immaculately tabulated vicinity)invei-
gles a few mildly curious rai
-ned on people(both male and female
created He

then,   And every beast of the field

I I I

"next to of course god america i
love you land of the pilgrims' and so forth oh
say can you see by the dawn's early my
country 'tis of centuries come and go
and are no more what of it we should worry
in every language even deafanddumb
thy sons acclaim your glorious name by gorry
by jingo by gee by gosh by gum
why talk of beauty what could be more beautiful than these heroic happy dead
who rushed like lions to the roaring slaughter
they did not stop to think they died instead
then shall the voice of liberty be mute?"

He spoke. And drank rapidly a glass of water

I V

    it's jolly
    odd what pops into
    your jolly tête when the
    jolly shells begin dropping jolly fast you
    hear the rrmp and
    then nearerandnearerandNEARER
    and before
    you can

    !

    & we're

    NOT
    (oh—
    —i say

    that's jolly odd
    old thing, jolly
    odd, jolly
    jolly odd isn't
    it jolly odd.

V

look at this)
a 75 done
this nobody would
have believed
would they no
kidding this was my particular

pal
funny aint
it we was
buddies
i used to

know
him lift the
poor cuss
tenderly this side up handle

with care
fragile
and send him home

to his old mother in
a new nice pine box

(collect

VI

first Jock he
was kilt a handsome
man and James and
next let me
see yes Will that was
cleverest
he was kilt and my youngest
boy was kilt last with
the big eyes i loved like you can't
imagine Harry was o
god kilt he was kilt everybody was kilt

they called them the kilties

VII

lis
-ten

you know what i mean when
the first guy drops you know
everybody feels sick or
when they throw in a few gas
and the oh baby shrapnel
or my feet getting dim freezing or
up to your you know what in water or
with the bugs crawling right all up
all everywhere over you all me everyone
that's been there knows what
i mean a god damned lot of
people don't and never
never
will know,
they don't want

to
no

VIII

come, gaze with me upon this dome
of many coloured glass, and see
his mother's pride, his father's joy,
unto whom duty whispers low

"thou must!" and who replies "I can!"
—yon clean upstanding well dressed boy
that with his peers full oft hath quaffed
the wine of life and found it sweet—

a tear within his stern blue eye,
upon his firm white lips a smile,
one thought alone: to do or die
for God for country and for Yale

above his blond determined head
the sacred flag of truth unfurled,
in the bright heyday of his youth
the upper class American

unsullied stands, before the world:
with manly heart and conscience free,
upon the front steps of her home
by the high minded pure young girl

much kissed, by loving relatives
well fed, and fully photographed
the son of man goes forth to war
with trumpets clap and syphilis

I X

16 heures
l'Etoile

the communists have fine Eyes

some are young some old none
look alike the flics rush
batter the crowd sprawls collapses
singing knocked down trampled the kicked by
flics rush(the

Flics, tidiyum, are
very tidiyum reassuringly similar,
they all have very tidiyum
mustaches, and very
tidiyum chins, and just above
their very tidiyum ears their
very tidiyum necks begin)
                                        let us add

that there are 50(fifty)flics for every
one(1)communist and
all the flics are very organically
arranged
and their nucleus(composed
of captains in freshly-creased
-uniforms with only-just-
shined buttons
tidiyum
before and behind)has a nucleolus:

the Prefect of Police

(a dapper derbied
creature, swaggers daintily
twiddling
his tiny cane
and, mazurkas about tweak-
ing his wing collar pecking at his im

-peccable cravat directing being
shooting his cuffs
saluted everywhere saluting
reviewing processions of minions
tappingpeopleontheback

"allezcirculez")

—my   he's brave . . . .
the
communists pick
up themselves friends
& their hats legs &

arms brush dirt coats
smile looking hands
spit blood teeth

the Communists have(very)fine eyes
(which stroll hither and thither through the
evening in bruised narrow questioning faces)

X

my sweet old etcetera
aunt lucy during the recent

war could and what
is more did tell you just
what everybody was fighting

for,
my sister

isabel created hundreds
(and
hundreds)of socks not to
mention shirts fleaproof earwarmers

etcetera wristers etcetera, my
mother hoped that

i would die etcetera
bravely of course my father used
to become hoarse talking about how it was
a privilege and if only he
could meanwhile my

self etcetera lay quietly
in the deep mud et

cetera
(dreaming,
et
   cetera, of
Your smile
eyes knees and of your Etcetera)

Three

I

now that fierce few
flowers(stealthily)
in the alive west
begin

requiescat this six
feet of Breton big good
body, which terminated
in fists hair wood

erect cursing hatless who
(bent by wind)slammed hard-
over the tiller;clattered
forward skidding in outrageous

sabots language trickling
pried his black
mouth with fat jibing
lips,

once upon a
(that is
over: and the sea heaving
indolent colourless forgets)time

Requiescat.
carry
carefully the blessed large silent him
into nibbling final worms

I I

Among

       these
            red pieces of
day(against which and
quite silently hills
made of blueandgreen paper

scorchbend ingthem
-selves-U
pcurv E,into:
              anguish(clim
b)ing
s-p-i-r-a-
l
  and,disappear)
                Satanic and blasé

a black goat lookingly wanders

There is nothing left of the world but
into this noth
ing il treno per
Roma si-gnori?
jerk.
ilyr,ushes

III

it is winter a moon in the afternoon
and warm air turning into January darkness up
through which sprouting gently, the cathedral
leans its dreamy spine against thick sunset

i perceive in front of our lady a ring of people
a brittle swoon of centrifugally expecting
faces clumsily which devours a man, three cats,
five white mice, and a baboon.

O a monkey with a sharp face waddling carefully
the length of this padded pole; a monkey attached
by a chain securely to this always talking
individual, mysterious witty hatless.

Cats which move smoothly from neck to neck of bottles, cats
smoothly willowing out and in between bottles, who step smoothly
and rapidly along this pole over five squirming
mice; or leap through hoops of fire, creating smoothness.

People stare, the drunker applaud
while twilight takes the sting out of the vermilion
jacket of nodding hairy Jacqueline who is given a mouse
to hold lovingly,

our lady what do you think of this? Do your proud fingers and
your arms tremble remembering something squirming fragile
and which had been presented unto you by a mystery?
. . . the cathedral recedes into weather without answering

I V

candles and

Here Comes a glass box
which the exhumed
hand of Saint Ignatz miraculously
inhabits. (people tumble
down. people crumble to their
knees. people
begin crossing people)and

hErE cOmEs a glass box:
surrounded by priests
moving in fifty colours
,sensuously

(the crowd
howls faintly
blubbering pointing

see
yes)
It
here
comes

A Glass
Box and incense with

and oh sunlight—
the crash of the
colours(of the oh
silently
striding)priests-and-
slowly,al,ways;procession:and

Enters

this
      church.

toward which The
Expectant stutter(upon artificial limbs,
with faces like defunct geraniums)

V

will out of the kindness of their hearts a few philosophers tell me
what am i doing on top of this hill at Calchidas, in the sunlight?
down ever so far on the beach below me a little girl in white spins,tumbles;
    rolling in sand.
across this water,crowding tints:browns and whites shoving,the dotting
    millions of windows of thousands of houses—Lisboa. Like the crackle
    of a typewriter,in the afternoon sky.
goats and sheep are driven by somebody along a curve of road which eats
    into a pink cliff back and up leaning out of yellowgreen water.

they are building a house down there by the sea,in the afternoon.

rapidly a reddish ant travels my fifth finger.
a bird chirps in a tree,somewhere nowhere
and a little girl in white is tumbling
in sand
        Clouds over
me are like bridegrooms

Naked and luminous

           (here the absurd I; life, to peer and wear clothes.
           i am altogether foolish, i suddenly make a fist
           out of ten fingers
voices rise from down ever so far—
hush.
    Sunlight,
        there are old men behind me I tell you;several,incredible,
        sleepy

V I

but observe; although
once is never the beginning of
enough, is it(i do not pretend
to know the reason any more than.)But look:up-

raising, hoisting, a little
perhaps that and this, deftly
propping on smallest hands
the slim hinging you
                              —because
it's five o'clock

and these(i notice)trees winterbrief surly old
gurgle a nonsense of sparrows, the cathedral
shudders blackening;
the sky is washed with tone

now for a moon
to squat in first darkness
—a little moon thinner than

memory

faint
-er
      than all the whys
which lurk
between your naked shoulderblades.—Here

comes a stout fellow in a blouse
just outside this window, touching the glass

boxes one by one with his magic
stick(in which a willing
bulb of flame bubbles)
                              see

here and here they explode
silently into crocuses of brightness. (That is enough
of life, for you. I understand. Once
again. . . .)sliding

a little downward, embrace me with your body's suddenly
curving entire warm questions

VII

sunlight was over
our mouths fears hearts lungs arms hopes feet hands

under us the unspeaking Mediterranean bluer
than we had imagined
a few cries drifting through
high air
a sail a fishing boat somebody an invisible spectator,
maybe certain nobodies laughing faintly

playing moving far below us

perhaps one villa caught like pieces
of a kite in the trees, here
and here reflecting
sunlight
(everywhere sunlight keen complete
silent

and everywhere you your kisses your flesh mind breathing
beside under around myself)
      by and by

a fat colour reared itself against the sky and the sea

. . . finally your eyes knew
me, we smiled to each other, releasing lay, watching
(sprawling, in
grass upon a
cliff) what had been something
else carefully slowly fatally turning into ourselves . . .

while in the very middle of fire all

the world becoming bright and little melted.

Four

I

the moon looked into my window
it touched me with its small hands
and with curling infantile
fingers it understood my eyes cheeks mouth
its hands(slipping)felt of my necktie wandered
against my shirt and into my body the
sharp things fingered tinily my heart life

the little hands withdrew, jerkily, themselves

quietly they began playing with a button
the moon smiled she
let go my vest and crept
through the window
she did not fall
she went creeping along the air
                    over houses
                            roofs

And out of the east toward
her a fragile light bent gatheringly

II

if being mortised with a dream
myself speaks

(whispering,
suggesting that our souls
inhabit whatever is between them)
knowing my lips hands the way i move
my habits laughter

i say
you will perhaps pardon,
possibly you will comprehend. and how
this has arrived your mind may guess

if at sunset
it should, leaning against me, smile;
or(between dawn and twilight)giving

your eyes, present me also
with the terror of shrines

which noone has suspected(but
wherein silently
always
are kneeling the various deaths
which are your lover lady: together with what keen
innumerable lives he has not lived.

III

here's a little mouse)and
what does he think about, i
wonder as over this
floor(quietly with

bright eyes)drifts(nobody
can tell because
Nobody knows, or why
jerks Here &, here,
gr(oo)ving the room's Silence)this like
a littlest
poem a
(with wee ears and see?

tail frisks)
                    (gonE)
"mouse",
            We are not the same you and

i, since here's a little he
or is
it It
?   (or was something we saw in the mirror)?

therefore we'll kiss; for maybe
what was Disappeared
into ourselves
who   (look).   ,startled

IV

but if i should say
goodmorning trouble adds
up all sorts of quickly
things on the slate of that
nigger's
face(but

If i should say thankyouverymuch

mr rosenbloom picks strawberries
with beringed hands)but if

i Should say solong my
tailor
chuckles

like a woman in a dream(but if i
should say
Now the all saucers
but cups if begin to spoons dance every-

should where say over the damned table and we
hold lips Eyes everything
hands you know what
happens)but if i should,
Say,

V

in spite of everything
which breathes and moves, since Doom
(with white longest hands
neatening each crease)
will smooth entirely our minds

—before leaving my room
i turn, and(stooping
through the morning)kiss
this pillow, dear
where our heads lived and were.

VI

you are not going to, dear.   You are not going to and
i but that doesn't in the least matter.   The big
fear Who held us deeply in His fist is

no longer, can you imagine it
i can't which doesn't matter
and what does is possibly this dear, that we may resume
impact with the inutile collide

once more with the imaginable, love, and eat sunlight(do
you believe it?   i begin to and that doesn't matter)which

i suggest teach us a new terror always
which shall brighten
carefully these things we consider life.
Dear i put my eyes into you but that doesn't matter
further than of old

because you fooled the doctors, i touch you with hopes and
words and with so and so: we are together, we will
kiss or smile or move.   It's different too isn't it

different dear from moving as we, you
and i, used to move when i thought you were going to(but
that doesn't matter)
when you thought you were going to America.
                                                    Then

moving was a matter of not keeping still; we were
two alert lice in the blond hair of nothing

VII

since feeling is first
who pays any attention
to the syntax of things
will never wholly kiss you;

wholly to be a fool
while Spring is in the world

my blood approves,
and kisses are a better fate
than wisdom
lady i swear by all flowers. Don't cry
—the best gesture of my brain is less than
your eyelids' flutter which says

we are for each other: then
laugh, leaning back in my arms
for life's not a paragraph

And death i think is no parenthesis

VIII

some ask praise of their fellows
but i being otherwise
made compose curves
and yellows, angles or silences
to a less erring end)

myself is sculptor of
your body's idiom:
the musician of your wrists;
the poet who is afraid
only to mistranslate

a rhythm in your hair,
(your fingertips
the way you move)
                        the

painter of your voice—
beyond these elements

remarkably nothing is. . . . therefore,lady
am i content should any
by me carven thing provoke
your gesture possibly or

any painting(for its own

reason)in your lips
slenderly should create one least smile
(shyly
if a poem should lift to
me the distinct country of your
eyes, gifted with green twilight)

I X

supposing i dreamed this)
only imagine, when day has thrilled
you are a house around which
i am a wind—

your walls will not reckon how
strangely my life is curved
since the best he can do
is to peer through windows, unobserved

—listen, for(out of all
things)dream is noone's fool;
if this wind who i am prowls
carefully around this house of you

love being such, or such,
the normal corners of your heart
will never guess how much
my wonderful jealousy is dark

if light should flower:
or laughing sparkle from
the shut house(around and around
which a poor wind will roam

X

you are like the snow only
purer fleeter, like the rain
only sweeter frailer you

whom certain
flowers resemble but trembling(cowards
which fear
to miss within your least gesture the hurting
skill which lives)and since

nothing lingers
beyond a little instant,
along with rhyme and with laughter
O my lady
(and every brittle marvelous breathing thing)

since i and you are on our ways to dust

of your fragility
(but chiefly of your smile,
most suddenly which is
of love and death a marriage) you give me

courage
so that against myself
the sharp days slobber in vain:

Nor am i afraid that
this, which we call autumn, cleverly
dies and over the ripe world wanders with
a near and careful
smile in his mouth (making

everything suddenly old and with his awkward eyes
pushing
sleep under and thoroughly
into all beautiful things)

winter, whom Spring shall kill

XI

because
you go away i give roses who
will advise even yourself, lady
in the most certainly (of what we
everywhere do not touch) deep
things;
       remembering ever so
tinily these, your crisp
eyes actually shall contain new faeries

(and if your slim lips are amused, no wisest

painter of fragile
Marys will understand
how smiling may be made as
skilfully.)   But carry
also, with that indolent and with
this flower wholly whom you do
not ever fear,
                    me in your heart

softly; not all
but the beginning

of mySelf

XII

you being in love
will tell who softly asks in love,

am i separated from your body smile brain hands merely
to become the jumping puppets of a dream?   oh i mean:
entirely having in my careful how
careful arms created this at length
inexcusable, this inexplicable pleasure—you go from several
persons: believe me that strangers arrive
when i have kissed you into a memory
slowly, oh seriously
—that since and if you disappear

solemnly
myselves
ask "life, the question how do i drink dream smile

and how do i prefer this face to another and
why do i weep eat sleep—what does the whole intend"
they wonder.   oh and they cry "to be, being, that i am alive
this absurd fraction in its lowest terms
with everything cancelled
but shadows
—what does it all come down to?   love?   Love
if you like and i like, for the reason that i
hate people and lean out of this window is love, love
and the reason that i laugh and breathe is oh love and the reason

that i do not fall into this street is love."

XIII

Nobody wears a yellow
flower in his buttonhole
he is altogether a queer fellow
as young as he is old

when autumn comes,
who twiddles his white thumbs
and frisks down the boulevards

without his coat and hat

—(and i wonder just why that
should please him or i wonder what he does)

and why(at the bottom of this trunk,
under some dirty collars)only a
moment
(or
was it perhaps a year)ago i found staring

me in the face a dead yellow small rose

XIV

it is so long since my heart has been with yours

shut by our mingling arms through
a darkness where new lights begin and
increase,
since your mind has walked into
my kiss as a stranger
into the streets and colours of a town—

that i have perhaps forgotten
how, always(from
these hurrying crudities
of blood and flesh)Love
coins His most gradual gesture,

and whittles life to eternity

—after which our separating selves become museums
filled with skilfully stuffed memories

XV

i am a beggar always
who begs in your mind

(slightly smiling, patient, unspeaking
with a sign on his
breast
BLIND)yes i

am this person of whom somehow
you are never wholly rid(and who

does not ask for more than
just enough dreams to
live on)
          after all, kid

you might as well
toss him a few thoughts

a little love preferably,
anything which you can't
pass off on other people: for
instance a
plugged promise—

then he will maybe(hearing something
fall into his hat)go wandering
after it with fingers; till having

found
what was thrown away
                    himself
taptaptaps out of your brain, hopes, life

to(carefully turning a
corner)never bother you any more.

XVI

if within tonight's erect
everywhere of black muscles fools
a weightless slowness(deftly

muting the world's texture with drifted

gifts of featheriest slenderness and
how gradually which descending are suddenly
received)or by doomfull connivance

accurately thither and hither myself

struts unremembered(rememberingly
with in both pockets curled hands moves)
why then toward morning he is a ghost whom

assault these whispering fists of hail

(and a few windows awaken certain faces
busily horribly blunder through new light
hush we are made of the same thing as perhaps

nothing,he murmurs carefully lying down)

XVII

how this uncouth enchanted
person, arising from a
restaurant, looks breathes or moves
—climbing(past light after
light)to turn, disappears

the very swift and
invisibly living
rhythm of your Heart possibly

will understand;
or why(in

this most exquisite of cities)all
of the long night a fragile imitation of
(perhaps)myself carefully wanders
streets dark and, deep

with rain . . . .

(he, slightly whom or
cautiously this person

and this imitation resemble,
descends into the earth with the year
a cigarette between his ghost-lips

gradually)
remembering badly, softly
your
kissed thrice suddenly smile

XVIII

i go to this window

just as day dissolves
when it is twilight(and
looking up in fear

i see the new moon
thinner than a hair)

making me feel
how myself has been coarse and dull
compared with you, silently who are
and cling
to my mind always

But now she sharpens and becomes crisper
until i smile with knowing
—and all about
herself

the sprouting largest final air

plunges
       inward with hurled
downward thousands of enormous dreams

Five

I

after all white horses are in bed

will you walking beside me, my very lady,
if scarcely the somewhat city
wiggles in considerable twilight

touch (now) with a suddenly unsaid

gesture lightly my eyes?
And send life out of me and the night
absolutely into me. . . . a wise
and puerile moving of your arm will
do suddenly that

      will do
more than heroes beautifully in shrill
armour colliding on huge blue horses,
and the poets looked at them, and made verses,

through the sharp light cryingly as the knights flew.

II

touching you i say (it being Spring
and night) "let us go a very little beyond
the last road—there's something to be found"

and smiling you answer "everything
turns into something else, and slips away. . . .
(these leaves are Thingish with moondrool
and i'm ever so very little afraid")
i say
"along this particular road the moon if you'll
notice follows us like a big yellow dog. You

don't believe? look back. (Along the sand
behind us, a big yellow dog that's . . . . now it's red
a big red dog that may be owned by who
knows)
only turn a little your. so. And

there's the moon, there is something faithful and mad"

III

along the brittle treacherous bright streets
of memory comes my heart,singing like
an idiot,whispering like a drunken man

who(at a certain corner,suddenly)meets
the tall policeman of my mind.
awake
being not asleep,elsewhere our dreams began
which now are folded:but the year completes
his life as a forgotten prisoner

—"Ici?"—"Ah non, mon chéri; il fait trop froid"—
they are gone:along these gardens moves a wind bringing
rain and leaves,filling the air with fear
and sweetness . . . . pauses. (Halfwhispering . . . . halfsinging

stirs the always smiling chevaux de bois)

when you were in Paris we met here

IV

our touching hearts slenderly comprehend
(clinging as fingers, loving one another
gradually into hands) and bend
into the huge disaster of the year:

like this most early single star which tugs

weakly at twilight, caught in thickening fear
our slightly fingering spirits starve and smother;
until autumn abruptly wholly hugs

our dying silent minds, which hand in hand
at some window try to understand
the
    (through pale miles of perishing air, haunted
with huddling infinite wishless melancholy,
suddenly looming) accurate undaunted

moon's bright third tumbling slowly

V

if i have made,my lady,intricate
imperfect various things chiefly which wrong
your eyes(frailer than most deep dreams are frail)
songs less firm than your body's whitest song
upon my mind—if i have failed to snare
the glance too shy—if through my singing slips
the very skillful strangeness of your smile
the keen primeval silence of your hair

—let the world say "his most wise music stole
nothing from death"—
                    you only will create
(who are so perfectly alive)my shame:
lady through whose profound and fragile lips
the sweet small clumsy feet of April came

into the ragged meadow of my soul.

W

(ViVa)

W

(ɛViV)

I

,mean-
hum
a)now

(nit
y unb
uria

ble fore(hurry
into
heads are
legs think wrists

argue)short(eyes do
bang hands angle
scoot bulbs marry a become)
ened
(to is

see!so
long door
golf slam bridge train shriek
chewing whistles hugest
to
morrow from smiles sin

k
ingly ele
vator glide pinn
)pu(
acle to

rubber)tres(plants how grin
ho)cen(tel
und
ead the

not stroll
living spawn imitate)ce(re
peat

credo fais do
do neighbours re babies
                                        while;

I I

oil tel duh woil doi sez
dooyuh unnurs tanmih eesez pullih nizmus tash,oi
dough un giv uh shid oi sez. Tom
oidoughwuntuh doot,butoiguttuh
braikyooz,datswut eesez tuhmih. (Nowoi askyuh
woodundat maik yurarstoin
green? Oilsaisough.)—Hool
spairruh luckih? Thangzkeed. Mairsee.
Muh jax awl gawn. Fur Croi saik
ainnoughbudih gutnutntuhplai?
                              HAI

yoozwidduhpoimnuntwaiv un duhyookuhsumpnruddur
givusuhtoonunduhphugnting

I I I

the surely

Cued
motif smites truly to Beautifully
retire through its english

the Forwardflung backwardSpinning hoop returns fasterishly
whipped the top leaps bounding upon other tops to caroming
off persist displacing Its own and their Lives who
grow slowly and first into different deaths

Concentric geometries of transparency slightly
joggled sink through algebras of proud

inwardlyness to collide spirally with iron arithmethics
and mesh witH
Which when both

march outward into the freezing fire of Thickness)points

uPDownwardishly
find everywheres noisecoloured
curvecorners gush silently perpetuating solids(More
fluid Than gas

I V

there are 6 doors.
Next door(but
four)gentlemen are trinightly entertained by a whore
who Talks in the daytime,when who

is asleep with only several
faces and a multitude of chins:next door
but three dwells;a(ghost)Who
screams Faintly always

who Is bluish;next
Door but two occupy a man
and his wife:Both very young noisily
who kiss throw silently things

Each at other(if not
quarrelling in a luxury of telescoped
languages)she smokes three
castles He looks jewish

,next door but One
a on Dirty bed Mangy from person Porous
sits years its of self fee(bly
Perpetually coughing And thickly spi)tting

But next door nobody
seems to live at present(l'on
parle de repapering;i
don't think so.maybe:somebody?)or,bedbugs

V

myself,walking in Dragon st
one fine August
night,i just
happened to meet

"how do you do" she smiling
said "thought you
were earning your living
or probably dead"

so Jones was murdered by
a man named Smith and
we sailed on the
Leviathan

VI

but mr can you maybe listen there 's
me &
some people
and others please
don't
confuse.Some

people

's future is toothsome like
(they got
pockets full may take a littl
e nibble now And then
bite)candy

others
fly,their;puLLing:bright
futures
against the deep sky in

May mine's tou
ching this crump
led cap mumble some
thing to oh no
body will
(can you give
a)listen to
who may

you

be
any
how?
down
to
smoking
found
Butts

VII

Space being(don't forget to remember)Curved
(and that reminds me who said o yes Frost
Something there is which isn't fond of walls)

an electromagnetic(now I've lost
the)Einstein expanded Newton's law preserved
conTinuum(but we read that beFore)

of Course life being just a Reflex you
know since Everything is Relative or

to sum it All Up god being Dead(not to

mention inTerred)
                    LONG LIVE that Upwardlooking
Serene Illustrious and Beatific
Lord of Creation,MAN:
                            at a least crooking
of Whose compassionate digit,earth's most terrific

quadruped swoons into billiardBalls!

VIII

(one fine day)

let's take the train
for because dear

whispered again
in never's ear
(i'm tho thcared

giggling lithped now
we muthn't pleathe
don't as pop weird
up her hot ow

you hurt tho nithe
steered his big was)
thither to thence
swore many a vow
but both made sense

in when's haymow
with young fore'er
(oh & by the way
asked sis breath
of brud breathe
how is aunt death

did always teethe

IX

y is a WELL KNOWN ATHLETE'S BRIDE

(lullaby)
& z

== an infrafairy of floating
ultrawrists who
lullabylullaby

(I could have been
You,You
might have been I)
          "?" quoth the

front;and there was yz
SHOT AND KILLED her
(in his arms)Self

       & Him
self in the hoe tell days are

teased:

    let(however)us
Walk very(therefore and)softly among one's own
memory(but)along perhaps the
By invisibilities spattered(or if

it may be socalled)memory
Of(without more ado about less
than nothing)

      2 boston
Dolls;found
with
Holes in each other

's lullaby and
other lulla wise by UnBroken
LULLAlullabyBY

          the She-in-him with
the He-in-her(&

both all hopped
        up)prettily
then which did
lie
Down,honestly

now who go(BANG(BANG

X

     thethe
the pink

Tartskids with
thecas-tanets
in5/4; Time

       chick.chick
but:that Mat isse like

-with-the-chinese-eyebrowsMan
gave me,A,

(peach
     a soft eyes syriansang asong tohim self
all

about the desertbyIts elf
             while) nextto
Mesmoked eleven camels
        !

and i got a Bad almond
chick.
     thepinkisht artskiDs . . .

     with thema Tiss eeyeb Rowspeach es
a soft desert smoked bad me whilepin Kishcam elscasta?netsits
Elf
   allaBout .
      (chic)
         -kchi
cK,

X I

   a
    mong crum
         bling people(a
   long ruined streets
   hither and)softly

thither between(tumb
ling)
    houses(as
the kno

wing spirit prowls,its
nose winces
before a dissonance of

Rish and Foses)
            until
                (finding one's self
at some distance from the
crooked town)a

harbour fools the sea(
while
        emanating the triple
starred

Hotel du Golf . . . that notable structure
or ideal edifice . . . situated or established
. . . far from the noise of waters
)one's

eye perceives
           (as the **ego** approaches)
painfully sterilized **contours;**
within

which
"ladies&gentlemen"
—under

glass—
are:
asking.

?each
oth?
er

rub,
!berq;
:uestions

XII

poor But TerFLY

went(flesh is grass)
from Troy,

n.y.
the way of(all
flesh is grass)with one "Paul"

a harvard boy
alas!
(who simply wor
shipped her)who

after not coming once in seven years explO
ded like a toy eloping to Ire(land must be
heav

en
FoR

my

motH)with a grass wid
OW

er who smelt rath
er like her fath
er who smelt rath

er(Er
camef
romth
AIR

XIII

remarked Robinson Jefferson

to Injustice Taughed
your story is so interested

but you make me laft
welates Wouldwoe Washington
to Lydia E. McKinley

when Buch tooked out his C.O.D.
Abe tucks it up back inley
clamored Clever Rusefelt
to Theodore Odysseus Graren't

we couldn't free the negro
because he ant
but Coolitch wiped his valley forge

with Sitting Bull's T.P.
and the duckbilled platitude lays & lays

and Lays aytash unee

XIV

what time is it i wonder never mind
consider rather heavenly things and but
the stars for instance everything is planned
next to that patch of darkness there 's a what
is it oh yes chair but not Cassiopeia's

might those be stockings dribbling from the table
all which seemed sweet deep and inexplicable
not being dollars toenails or ideas
thoroughly 's stolen(somewhere between

our unlighted hearts lust lurks
slovenly and homeless and when
a kiss departs our lips are made of thing

in beginning corners dawn smirks

and there's the moon, thinner than a watchspring

X V

well)here's looking at ourselves

two solids in(all
one it)
solution(of
course you must shake well)

indolently dreaming puzzling

over that one
oh just thinking it over
(at that just supposing
we had met and just
but you know

supposing we

just had let it go at
that)that
seems important doesn't
it and
doesn't that seem
puzzling but we both might have found the solution

of that in

the importance of the
fact that(in spite of the fact
that i and that
you had carefully
ourselves decided what this cathedral ought to

look like)it doesn't look

at
all like what you
and what i(of course)
carefully had decided oh

no(but

XVI

tell me not how electricity or
god was invented but
why(captured by a
policeman's majestic and buried eye)

the almost large he-
shaped object vomits cleverly
against a quai wall almost spray
-ing threecoloured puke over

this younger than
i am newspaper guy who refused
to shake hands with
ludendorf and your humble moving through the

gloominess of(try to
imagine)whispering
of a named
Krassin

XVII

FULL SPEED ASTERN)

m

usil(age)ini
sticks
tuh de mans

l

(hutch)hutchinson says sweet guinea
pigs do it it buy uh cupl un
wait

k

(relijinisde)o(peemuvdepipl)
marx okays jippymugun
roomur

j

            e(wut)
        hova
        in big cumbine wid

        i

        (check
        undublcheck)
        babbitt

    (GOD SAVE THE UNCOMMONWEALTH OF
              HUMANUSETTS

                XVIII

"Gay" is the captivating cognomen of a Young Woman of cambridge,
    mass.
to whom nobody seems to have mentioned ye olde freudian wish;
when i contemplate her uneyes safely ensconced in thick glass
you try if we are a gentleman not to think of(sh)

the world renowned investigator of paper sailors—argonauta argo
harmoniously being with his probably most brilliant pupil mated,
let us not deem it miraculous if their(so to speak)offspring has that largo
appearance of somebody who was hectocotyliferously propagated

when Miss G touched n.y. our skeleton stepped from his cupboard
gallantly offering to demonstrate the biggest best busiest city
and presently found himself rattling for that well known suburb
the bronx(enlivening an otherwise dead silence with harmless quips, out
    of Briggs by Kitty)

arriving in an exhausted condition, i purchased two bags of lukewarm
    peanuts
with the dime which her mama had generously provided(despite courte-
    ous protestations)
and offering Miss Gay one(which she politely refused)set out gaily for
    the hyenas
suppressing my frank qualms in deference to her not inobvious perturba-
    tions

unhappily, the denizens of the zoo were that day inclined to be uncouthly
    erotic
more particularly the primates—from which with dignity square feet
    turned abruptly Miss Gay away:
"on the whole"(if you will permit a metaphor savouring slightly of the
    demotic)
Miss Gay had nothing to say to the animals and the animals had nothing
    to say to Miss Gay

during our return voyage, my pensive companion dimly remarked some-
    thing about "*stuffed*
fauna" being "very interesting" . . . we also discussed the possibility of
    rain. . .
in distant proximity to a Y.W.c.a. she suddenly luffed
—thanking me; and(stating that she hoped we might "meet again

sometime")vanished, gunwale awash. I thereupon loosened my collar
and dove for the nearest l; surreptitiously cogitating
the dictum of a new england sculptor(well on in life)re the helen moller
dancers, whom he considered "elevating—that is, if dancing CAN be ele-
    vating"

Miss(believe it or)Gay is a certain Young Woman unacquainted with the
    libido
and pursuing a course of instruction at radcliffe college, cambridge, mass.
i try if you are a gentleman not to sense something un poco putrido
when we contemplate her uneyes safely ensconced in thick glass

XIX

i will cultivate within
me scrupulously the Inimitable which
is loneliness,these unique dreams
never shall soil their raiment

with phenomena:such
being a conduct worthy of

more ponderous
wishes or
hopes less
tall than mine"(opening the windows)

"and there is a philosophy" strictly at
which instant(leaped
into the

street)this deep immediate mask and
expressing "as for myself,because i
am slender and fragile
i borrow contact from that you and from

this you sensations,imitating a few fatally

exquisite"(pulling Its shawl carefully around
it)"things i mean the
Rain is no respecter of persons
the snow doesn't give a soft white
damn Whom it touches

X X

but granted that it's nothing paradoxically enough beyond mere personal

pride which tends to compel me to decline to admit i've died)
seeing your bald intellect collywobbling on its feeble stem is

believing science$=(2b)^{-n}$ herr professor m

X X I

helves surling out of eakspeasies per(reel)hapsingly
proregress heandshe-ingly people
trickle curselaughgroping shrieks bubble
squirmwrithed staggerful unstrolls collaps ingly
flash a of-faceness stuck thumblike into pie
is traffic this recalls hat gestures bud
plumptumbling hand voices Eye Doangivuh suddenly immense impotently Eye Doancare Eye
And How replies the upsquirtingly careens
the to collide flatfooting with Wushyuhname
a girl-flops to the Geddup curb leans
carefully spewing into her own Shush Shame

as(out from behind Nowhere)creeps the deep thing
everybody sometimes calls morning

XXII

Lord John Unalive(having a fortune of fifteengrand
£
thanks to the socalled fact that maost faolks rally demannd canned
saounds)
gloats
upon the possession of quotes keltyer close
" "

aureally(yawning while all the dominoes)fall:down;in,rows

XXIII

    buncha hardboil guys frum duh A.C. fulla
    hooch kiddin eachudder bout duh clap an
    talkin big how dey could kill
    sixereight cops—"I sidesteps im an draws
    back huly jeezus"—an—"my
    specialty is takin fellers' goils away
    frum dem"—"somebody hung uh gun on
    Marcus"—"duh Swede rolls down tree flights an Sam
    begins boxin im on duh
    koib"—you
    know
    alotta sweet bull like dat
                           . . . suddenly
    i feels so lonely fer duh good ole days we
    spent in '18 kickin duh guts outa dem
    doity frogeaters an humpin duh
    swell janes on
    duh boollevares an wid tears
    streamin down my face i hauls
    out uh flask an offers it tuh duh whole gang accrost
    duh table—"fellers
    have some
    on
    me"—dey was petrified.

    De room swung roun an crawled up into
    itself,
    an awful big light squoits down my spine like
    i was dead er sumpn:next i

knows me(er
somebody is sittin in uh green
field watchin four crows drop into
sunset,playin uh busted harmonica

XXIV

from the cognoscenti

bingbongwhom chewchoo
laugh dingle nails personally
bung loamhome picpac
obviously scratches tomorrowlobs

wholeagainst you gringlehow
exudes thursday fasters
by button of whisper sum blinked
he belowtry eye nowbrow

sangsung née whitermuch grab
sicksilk soak sulksuck whim
poke if inch dimmer twist on
permament and slap tremendous

sorrydaze bog triperight
election who so thumb o'clock
asters miggle dim a ram
flat hombre sin bangaroom

slim guesser goose pin yessir wheel
no sendwisp ben jiffyclaus
bug fainarain wee celibate
amaranth clutch owch

so chuck slop hight evolute
my eerily oh gargle
to jip hug behemoth
truly pseudo yours podia

of radarw leschin

X X V

ohld song

you Know
a fly and
his reflection walking upon

a mirror this is
friday 1

what

3 a fly
&

her his Its image
strutting(very
jerkily)not toucH-

ing because separated by an impregnable

Because(amount of inter
-vening)anyway You
know Separated what
i Mean

    (oweld song by
    ;neither you nor i and

by the way)

    ,which is not fly

X X V I

murderfully in midmost o.c.an

launch we a Hyperluxurious Supersieve
(which Ultima Thule Of Plumbing shall receive

the philophilic name S.S. VAN MERDE)

having first put right sleuthfully aboard
all to—mendaciously speaking—a man

wrongers who write what they are dine to live

XXVII

the first president to be loved by his
bitterest enemies" is dead

the only man woman or child who wrote
a simple declarative sentence with seven grammatical
errors "is dead"
beautiful Warren Gamaliel Harding
"is" dead
he's
"dead"
if he wouldn't have eaten them Yapanese Craps

somebody might hardly never not have been
unsorry,perhaps

XXVIII

serene immediate silliest and whose
vast one function being to enter a Toy and
emerging(believably enlarged)make how
many stopped millions of female hard for their
millions of stopped male to look at(now
-fed infantile eyes drooling unmind
grim yessing childflesh perpetually acruise
and her quick way of slowly staring and such hair)
the Californian handpicked thrill mechanically
packed and released for all this very diminishing
vicarious ughhuh world(the pertly papped
muchmouthed)her way of beginningly finishing
(and such hair)the expensively democratic tyrannically
dumb

Awake,chaos:we have napped.

XXIX

in a middle of a room
stands a suicide
sniffing a Paper rose
smiling to a self

"somewhere it is Spring and sometimes
people are in real:imagine
somewhere real flowers,but
I can't imagine real flowers for if I

could,they would somehow
not Be real"
(so he smiles
smiling)"but I will not

everywhere be real to
you in a moment"
The is blond
with small hands

"& everything is easier
than I had guessed everything would
be;even remembering the way who
looked at whom first,anyhow dancing"

(a moon swims out of a cloud
a clock strikes midnight
a finger pulls a trigger
a bird flies into a mirror)

XXX

i sing of Olaf glad and big
whose warmest heart recoiled at war:
a conscientious object-or

his wellbelovéd colonel(trig
westpointer most succinctly bred)
took erring Olaf soon in hand;
but—though an host of overjoyed
noncoms(first knocking on the head
him)do through icy waters roll
that helplessness which others stroke
with brushes recently employed
anent this muddy toiletbowl,
while kindred intellects evoke
allegiance per blunt instruments—
Olaf(being to all intents
a corpse and wanting any rag
upon what God unto him gave)
responds,without getting annoyed
"I will not kiss your f.ing flag"

straightway the silver bird looked grave
(departing hurriedly to shave)

but—though all kinds of officers
(a yearning nation's blueeyed pride)
their passive prey did kick and curse
until for wear their clarion
voices and boots were much the worse,
and egged the firstclassprivates on
his rectum wickedly to tease
by means of skilfully applied
bayonets roasted hot with heat—
Olaf(upon what were once knees)
does almost ceaselessly repeat
"there is some s. I will not eat"

our president,being of which
assertions duly notified
threw the yellowsonofabitch
into a dungeon,where he died

Christ(of His mercy infinite)
i pray to see;and Olaf,too

preponderatingly because
unless statistics lie he was
more brave than me:more blond than you.

XXXI

memory believes
fragrance of a town(whose
dormers choke
and snore the steeples writhe with

rain)faces(at windows)do not
speak and are ghosts or
huddled in the darkness of
cafés people drink

smile if here there(like lopsided
imaginations)
filled with newly murdered
flowers whispering barns

bulge a tiniest street or
three contains these prettiest
deaths without effort while
hungering churches(topped

with effigies of crowing
gold)nuzzle against summer
thunder(together)smell only
such blue slender hands of god

XXXII

Wing Wong,uninterred at twice
fortyeight,succeeded in producing

sixtyfour maxims

whose)centripetal wisdom in
thirtytwo seconds centrifugally
is refuted by these(

particularly belonging to
a
retired
general)sixteen years

of rapid
animal whose swir
-ling(not too frequently
)skirt exhumes(which
buries again quick-

ly its
self in)while
a transparent blouse
even recklessly
juggles the jouncing
fruit of eager bosoms"
                              Wing

  Wong

XXXIII

innerly

UningstrolL
(stamens&pistil
                    silent
A s groupingThe
6around one
darks to 7th s
                    o howpale)
bluedmufFletomben

                              outerly

jeT
ting lip ssixs ting
sWervesca
rletlycaR v Ingharness
Of
curvish(

,males await she
patiently 1

)littlecrownGrave
whose whorlclown of spreadnessed bE
rich from-soft quits(now)ly
Comes;
:lush
ly-smootHdumb droopnew-gree

N.lyestmostsaresl e A v e S

X X X I V

don't cries to please my
mustn't broke)life Is
like that please stroke

for now stroke answers(but
now don't you're hurting o
Me please you're killing)death

is like now That please
squirtnowing for
o squirting we're replies(at

which now O fear turned o Now
handspring trans
forming it

self int
o eighteen)Don't
(for)Please(tnights,on whose for

eheads shone
eternal pleasedon't;
rising:from the Shall.

XXXV

what is strictly fiercely and wholly dies
his impeccable feathered with green facts
preening solemnity ignoring,through
its indolent lascivious caring eyes

watches;truly,curvingly while reacts
(sharp now with blood now accurately wan)
keenly,to dreamings more than truth untrue,

the best mouth i have seen on any man—
a little fluttering,at the enchanted dike
of whose lean lips,hovers how slenderly
the illustrious unknown

                    (warily as
their master's spirit stooping,Crusoelike
examines fearingly and tenderly

a recent footprint in the sand of was)

XXXVI

        sunset)edges become swiftly
        corners(Besides
        which,i note how
        fatally toward

        twilight the a little
        tilted streets spill lazily
        multitudes out of final

        towers;captured:in
        the narrow light

    of

    inverno)this
    is the season of
    crumbling & folding
    hopes,hark;feet(fEEt
    f-e-e-t-noWheregoingaLwaYS

XXXVII

          how
ses humble.

Over thin earths chatterish

strut cuddle & shrink:
as through immediately
yeswind-faces peer

skies;whiteLy
are which stumbling eyes which
why in(thundering)by
When eaten

spaces grouse rocket know
quite,

slightly or
how at the yearhour tree-
    spires shout appalling

              deathmoney into
                          spiralS
                                and
Now(comes

un,

    season of in:wardly
of him(every)

who does
(where)not move
;is

    .crowned the with shrill
Nonleaf daemons and large The downlife gods of
shut
)

XXXVIII

n(o)w

    the
how
   dis(appeared cleverly)world

iS Slapped:with;liGhtninG
!

 at
which(shal)lpounceupcrackw(ill)jumps

of
  THuNdeRB
        loSSo!M iN
-visiblya mongban(gedfrag-
ment ssky?wha tm)eani ngl(essNessUn
rolli)ngl yS troll s(who leO v erd)oma insCol

Lide.!high
      n,o ; w :
           theraIncomIng

o all the roofs roar
         drownInsound(
&
(we(are like)dead
)Whoshout(Ghost)atOne(voiceless)O
ther or im)
   pos
   sib(ly as
   leep)
     But l!ook—
        s

   U

     n:starT birDs(lEAp)Openi ng
t hing ; s(
—sing
)all are aLl(cry alL See)o(ver All)Th(e grEEn

?eartH)N,ew

XXXIX

An(fragrance)Of

(Begins)
millions

Of Tints(and)
&
(grows)Slowly(slowly)Voyaging

tones intimate tumult
(Into)bangs
minds into
dream(An)quickly

Not

un deux trois
der
        die

Stood(apparition.)
WITH(THE ROUND AIR IS FILLED)OPENING

X L

  thou

     firsting a hugeness of twi
          -light
  pale
    beyond soft-
  liness than dream more sing

  (buoyant & who
  silently shall to rea- disa)

  ular,

    (ppear ah!Star
      whycol

our
ed
shy lurch small invin

cible nod oc
cul
t ke
ylike writhe of brea

Thing

XLI

twi-
is -Light bird
ful
-ly dar
kness eats

a distance a
c(h)luck
(l)ing of just bells (touch)ing
?mind

(moon begins The
)
now,est hills er dream;new
.oh if

when:
&
a
nd O impercept i bl

XLII

structure,miraculous challenge,devout am

upward deep most invincible unthing
—stern sexual timelessness,outtowering
this noisy impotence of not and same

answer,beginning,ecstasy,to dare:
prouder than all mountains,more than all
oceans various
                    and while everywhere
beneath thee and about thyself a small
hoping insect,humanity,achieves
(moult beyond difficult moult)amazing doom
who standest as thou hast stood and thou shalt stand.

Nor any dusk but kneelingly believes
thy secret and each morning stoops to blend

her star with what huge merciful forms presume

XLIII

if there are any heavens my mother will(all by herself)have
one. It will not be a pansy heaven nor
a fragile heaven of lilies-of-the-valley but
it will be a heaven of blackred roses

my father will be(deep like a rose
tall like a rose)

standing near my

(swaying over her
silent)
with eyes which are really petals and see

nothing with the face of a poet really which
is a flower and not a face with
hands
which whisper
This is my beloved my

                         (suddenly in sunlight
he will bow,

& the whole garden will bow)

XLIV

i'd think "wonder

if" if
i were a
child "we can see a bat in this
twilight")
              there one is

look

how it goes   like   a dream

(and between houses,really a kind of
mouse)but he has little wings
and here's my
hotel this is the
door(opening it i

think things
which
were supposed to
be out of my
reach
        ,they are like
jam on the shelf everybody guessed

was too high

look

      (it's back again   there   therehere
And)i say "won't you"(remembering)
knowing that you
are afraid "go first" of dreams and little

bats & mice(and

                you,
you say "let's" going in
"take
hands" smiling "coming up
these dark stairs.

XLV

                    you
                  in win
                ter who sit
              dying thinking
            huddled behind dir
          ty glass mind muddled
        and cuddled by dreams(or some
      times vacantly gazing through un
    washed panes into a crisp todo of
    murdering uncouth faces which pass rap
  idly with their breaths.)"people are walking deaths
  in this season" think "finality lives up
  on them a little more openly than usual
  hither,thither who briskly busily carry the as
tonishing & spontaneous & difficult ugliness
  of themselves with a more incisive simplicity a
  more intensively brutal futility"And sit
          huddling dumbly behind three or two partly tran
        sparent panes which by some loveless trick sepa
      rate one stilled unmoving mind from a hun
        dred doomed hurrying brains(by twos
      or threes which fiercely rapidly
        pass with their breaths)in win
          ter you think,die slow
            ly "toc tic" as i
            have seen trees(in
            whose black bod
              ies leaves
              hide

XLVI

i met a man under the moon
on Sunday.
by way of saying
nothing he
smiled(but
just by the dirty collar of his

jacket were two glued uncarefully ears
in
that face a box of
skin lay eyes like
new tools)

whence i guessed that he also had climbed the pincian
to appreciate rome at nightfall;and because against this
wall his white sincere small
hands with their guessing fingers

did-not-move exquisitely
,like dead children
(if he had been playing a fiddle i had

been dancing:which is
why something about me reminded him of ourselves

as Nobody came slowly over the town)

XLVII

when rain whom fear
not children but men
speaks(among leaves Easily
through voices womenlike telling

of death love earth dark)

and thousand
thrusts squirms stars
Trees,swift each with its

Own motion deeply to wickedly

comprehend the innocently Doomed
brief all which somewhere is

fragrantly,

arrive
        (when
Rain comes;
predicating forever,assuming
the laughter of afterwards—
i spirally understand

What

touching means
or What does a hand
with your hair
in my imagination

XLVIII

come a little further—why be afraid—
here's the earliest star(have you a wish?)
touch me,
before we perish
(believe that not anything which has ever been
invented can spoil this or this instant)
kiss me a little:
the air
darkens and is alive—
o live with me in the fewness of
these colours;
alone who slightly
always are beyond the reach of death

and the English

XLIX

a light Out)
    & first of all foam

-like hair spatters creasing pillow
next everywhere hidinglyseek
no o god dear wait sh please o no O
3rd Findingest whispers understand
sobs bigly climb what(love being something possibly more intricate)i(breath
in breath)have nicknamed ecstasy and And

spills smile cheaply thick

—who therefore Thee(once and once only,Queen
among centuries universes between
Who out of deeplyness rose to undeath)

salute. and having worshipped for my doom
pass ignorantly into sleep's bright land

L

when hair falls off and eyes blur And
thighs forget(when clocks whisper
and night shouts)When minds
shrivel and hearts grow brittler every
Instant(when of a morning Memory stands,
with clumsily wilted fingers
emptying youth colour and what was
into a dirtied glass)Pills for Ills
(a recipe against Laughing Virginity Death)

then dearest the
way trees are Made leaves
open Clouds take sun mountains
stand And oceans do Not sleep matters
nothing;then(then the only hands so to speak are
they always which creep budgingly over some
numbered face capable of a largest nonglance the
least unsmile
or whatever weeds feel and fish think of)

L I

a clown's smirk in the skull of a baboon
(where once good lips stalked or eyes firmly stirred)
my mirror gives me,on this afternoon;
i am a shape that can but eat and turd
ere with the dirt death shall him vastly gird,
a coward waiting clumsily to cease
whom every perfect thing meanwhile doth miss;
a hand's impression in an empty glove,
a soon forgotten tune,a house for lease.
I have never loved you dear as now i love

behold this fool who,in the month of June,
having of certain stars and planets heard,
rose very slowly in a tight balloon
until the smallening world became absurd;
him did an archer spy(whose aim had erred
never)and by that little trick or this
he shot the aeronaut down,into the abyss
—and wonderfully i fell through the green groove
of twilight,striking into many a piece.
I have never loved you dear as now i love

god's terrible face,brighter than a spoon,
collects the image of one fatal word;
so that my life(which liked the sun and the moon)
resembles something that has not occurred:
i am a birdcage without any bird,
a collar looking for a dog,a kiss
without lips;a prayer lacking any knees
but something beats within my shirt to prove
he is undead who,living,noone is.
I have never loved you dear as now i love.

Hell(by most humble me which shall increase)
open thy fire! for i have had some bliss
of one small lady upon earth above;
to whom i cry,remembering her face,
i have never loved you dear as now i love

LII

it)It will it
Will come(we
being
unwound & gone into the ground)but

though

with wormS eyes
writhe amor(Though through

our hearts hugely squirm
roots)us
          ly;though
hither nosing lymoles cru.Ising

thither:t,ouch soft-ly me and eye(you
leSs

)ly(un
        der the mi
                  croscopic world's

whens,wheels;wonders:
murders.cries:hopes;
houses,clouds.kisses,
lice;headaches:ifs.

)
 yet shall
our Not to
be

deciphered
selves

merely Continue to experience

a neverish subchemistry of
alWays
)fiercely live whom on

Large Darkness And The Middle Of
The
E

a
r
t
H

LIII

breathe with me this fear
(which beyond night shall go)
remembering only dare
(Wholly consider how

these immaculate thin
things half daemon half
tree among sunset dream
acute from root to leaf)

but should voices(whom lure
an eagerest strict flame)
demand the metaphor
of our projectile am

tell such to murder time
(forgetting what's to know
wholly imagining fire)
only consider How

LIV

if i love You
(thickness means
worlds inhabited by roamingly
stern bright færies

if you love
me)distance is mind carefully
luminous with innumerable gnomes
Of complete dream

if we love each(shyly)
other,what clouds do or Silently
Flowers resembles beauty
less than our breathing

L V

speaking of love(of
which Who knows the
meaning;or how dreaming
becomes

if your heart's mine)i
guess a grassblade
Thinks beyond or
around(as poems are

made)Our picking it. this
caress that laugh
both quickly signify
life's only half(through

deep weather then
or none let's feel
all)mind in mind flesh
In flesh succeeding disappear

L V I

lady will you come with me into
the extremely little house of
my mind.   Clocks strike.   The

moon's round,through the window

as you see and really i have no
servants.   We could almost live

at the top of these stairs,there's a free
room.   We almost could go(you
and i)into a together whitely big
there is but if so or so

slowly i opened the window a
most tinyness,the moon(with white wig
and polished buttons)would take you away

—and all the clocks would run down the next day.

LVII

somewhere i have never travelled,gladly beyond
any experience,your eyes have their silence:
in your most frail gesture are things which enclose me,
or which i cannot touch because they are too near

your slightest look easily will unclose me
though i have closed myself as fingers,
you open always petal by petal myself as Spring opens
(touching skilfully,mysteriously)her first rose

or if your wish be to close me,i and
my life will shut very beautifully,suddenly,
as when the heart of this flower imagines
the snow carefully everywhere descending;

nothing which we are to perceive in this world equals
the power of your intense fragility:whose texture
compels me with the colour of its countries,
rendering death and forever with each breathing

(i do not know what it is about you that closes
and opens;only something in me understands
the voice of your eyes is deeper than all roses)
nobody,not even the rain,has such small hands

LVIII

is there a flower(whom
i meet anywhere
able to be and seem
so quite softly as your hair

what bird has perfect fear
(of suddenly me)like these
first deepest rare
quite who are your eyes

(shall any dream
come a more millionth mile
shyly to its doom
than you will smile)

LIX

my darling since
you and
i are thoroughly haunted by
what neither is any
echo of dream nor
any flowering of any

echo(but the echo
of the flower of

Dreaming)somewhere behind us
always trying(or sometimes trying under
us)to is it
find somehow(but O gracefully)a
we,entirely whose least

breathing may surprise
ourselves
            —let's then
despise what is not courage my

darling(for only Nobody knows
where truth grows why
birds fly and
especially who the moon is.

LX

because i love you)last night

clothed in sealace
appeared to me
your mind drifting
with chuckling rubbish
of pearl weed coral and stones;

lifted,and(before my
eyes sinking)inward,fled;softly
your face smile breasts gargled
by death:drowned only

again carefully through deepness to rise
these your wrists
thighs feet hands

poising
         to again utterly disappear;
rushing gently swiftly creeping
through my dreams last
night,all of your
body with its spirit floated
(clothed only in

the tide's acute weaving murmur

LXI

if you and i awakening

discover that(somehow
in the dark)this world has been
Picked,like a piece
of clover,from the green meadow of

time

lessness;quietly
         turning
toward me the
guessable mirrors which your eyes are

You will communicate a little

more than twice all that
so
gently
while we were asleep while
we were each other disappeared:but i

slightly

smiling,
gradually shall reenter the

singular kingdom

(sleep)
      .while some
thing else
kisses busily
a
memory,which how exquisitely
flutters in

the cornerless tomorrow

LXII

item:is

    Clumsily with of
what manshaped whimpered how
                  girllike
laughtering blocks when

builds
its invisibly skil
ful toyTown
which upups to dowNdown
(and only where remembers

look,
        this was of a child
's shy foot among cool ferns

)
  therefore togethering our

wholly lives Givehurling
with your my most
:locking

       foreverfully

blend
      we a universe of gulls'
drift Of thickly
           starhums wherefore

& wormSmile eternal;quite
perhaps as sternly
much not life nor stop as
a tear is darker than a mile.

LXIII

be unto love as rain is unto colour;create
me gradually(or as these emerging now
hills invent the air)
           breathe simply my each how
my trembling where my still unvisible when.   Wait

if i am not heart,because at least i beat
—always think i am gone like a sun which must go
sometimes,to make an earth gladly seem firm for you:
remember(as those pearls more than surround this throat)

i wear your dearest fears beyond their ceaselessness

(nor has a syllable of the heart's eager dim
enormous language loss or gain from blame or praise)
but many a thought shall die which was not born of dream
while wings welcome the year and trees dance(and i guess

though wish and world go down,one poem yet shall swim

LXIV

granted the all
                  saving our young kiss only
must unexist,solemnly and per rules
apparelling its soullessness by lonely
antics of ridiculous molecules)

nakedest(aiming for hugely the
ignorant most precise essential flame
never which waked)& perfectingly We

dive

      out of tinying time
                   (into supreme

Now:
       feeling memory shrink from such brief
selves as fiercely seek findingly new
textures of actual cool stupendous is

nor may truth opening encompass true)
while your contriving fate,my sharpening life

are(behind each no)touching every yes

LXV

but being not amazing:without love
separate,smileless—merely imagine your

sorrow a certain reckoning demands. . .

marvelling And what may have become of
with his gradual acute lusting glance
an alert clumsily foolishwise

(tracking the beast Tomorrow by her spoor)
over the earth wandering hunter whom you
knew once?

   what if(merely suppose)

mine should overhear and answer Who
with the useless flanks and cringing feet
is this(shivering pale naked very poor)
creature of shadow,that among first light

groping washes my nightmare from his eyes?

LXVI

nothing is more exactly terrible than
to be alone in the house,with somebody and
with something)
     You are gone. there is laughter

and despair impersonates a street

i lean from the window,behold ghosts,
         a man
hugging a woman in a park. Complete.

and slightly(why?or lest we understand)
slightly i am hearing somebody
coming up stairs,carefully
(carefully climbing carpeted flight after
carpeted flight. in stillness,climbing
the carpeted stairs of terror)

and continually i am seeing something

inhaling gently a cigarette(in a mirror

LXVII

put off your faces,Death:for day is over
(and such a day as must remember he
who watched unhands describe what mimicry,

with angry seasalt and indignant clover
marrying to themselves Life's animals)

but not darkness shall quite outmarch forever
—and i perceive,within transparent walls
how several smoothly gesturing stars are clever
to persuade even silence:therefore wonder

opens a gate;the prisoner dawn embraces

hugely some few most rare perfectly dear
(and worlds whirl beyond worlds:immortal yonder
collidingly absorbs eternal near)

day being come,Love,put on your faces

LXVIII

but if a living dance upon dead minds
why,it is love;but at the earliest spear
of sun perfectly should disappear
moon's utmost magic,or stones speak or one
name control more incredible splendor than
our merely universe,love's also there:
and being here imprisoned,tortured here
love everywhere exploding maims and blinds
(but surely does not forget,perish,sleep
cannot be photographed,measured;disdains
the trivial labelling of punctual brains. . .
—Who wields a poem huger than the grave?
from only Whom shall time no refuge keep
though all the weird worlds must be opened?
)Love

LXIX

so standing,our eyes filled with wind,and the
whining rigging over us,i implore you to
notice how the keen ship lifts(skilfully
like some bird which is all birds but more fleet)
herself against the air—and whose do you
suppose possibly are certain hands,terse
and invisible,with large first new stars
knitting the structure of distinct sunset

driving white spikes of silence into joists
hewn from hugest colour
                         (and which night hoists
miraculously above the always
beyond such wheres and fears or any when
unwondering immense directionless
horizon)
          —do you perhaps know these workmen?

LXX

here is the ocean,this is moonlight:say
that both precisely beyond either were—
so in darkness ourselves go,mind in mind

which is the thrilling least of all(for love's
secret supremely clothes herself with day)

i mean,should any curious dawn discuss
our mingling spirits,you would disappear
unreally;as this planet(understand)

forgets the entire and perpetual sea

—but if yourself consider wonderful
that your(how luminous)life toward twilight will
dissolve reintegrate beckon through me,
i think it is less wonderful than this

only by you my heart always moves

No Thanks

TO

Farrar & Rinehart
Simon & Schuster
Coward-McCann
Limited Editions
Harcourt, Brace
Random House
Equinox Press
Smith & Haas
Viking Press
Knopf
Dutton
Harper's
Scribner's
Covici, Friede

1

mOOn Over tOwns mOOn
whisper
less creature huge grO
pingness

whO perfectly whO
flOat
newly alOne is
dreamest

oNLY THE MooN o
VER ToWNS
SLoWLY SPRoUTING SPIR
IT

2

moon over gai
-té.a
sharp crone dodders be-
tween taxis swirl hues crowds mov
-ing ing ing
among who dreams whom mutterings dream &

:the moon over death over edgar the
moon
        over smellings of gently smell of deads
(lovers grip sprawl twitch lovers)
& one dog?piglike big!sorrows

always;finally and always,the iflike moon over moving
me—the
moon
m
ov—in
g
over(moving)you beautifully also;at

denfert the fat strongman has put
down his carpet from which rise slim curving mighty
children while a python over the way freezes
a serpent becomes a
rod smiles
the liontamer nearby hieroglyphs
soar dip
dip
soar equalling noise solemn

dolls re
-volve whirlswans rabbitsare:
swimswim
painted-with-horses-with-painted-
with eyes and the.m

oon over juillet moon over s
-unday

O:
m
o
o
n
o
  (ver no(w ove(r all;
                 o
ver pinkthisgreen acr)o)greenthatpink)
acrobata

mong
trees climbing on
A

pi llarofch airso vertheseu pstareth oseings
over
(a hard a
hard a girl a girl)sing
-ing ing(ing
sing)ing a soft a song a softishsongly

v
  o
   i
    c
      e o
        ver
(whi!tethatr?apidly
legthelessne sssuc kedt oward
black,this

)roUnd ingrOundIngly rouNdar(round)ounDing

                              ;ball
                              balll
                              ballll
                              balllll

3

that which we who're alive in spite of mirrors
(have died beyond the clock)we,of ourselves

who more a part are(less who are aware)

than of my books could even be your shelves
(that which we die for;not when or unless
if or to prove,imperfectly or since

but through spontaneous deft strictly horrors

which stars may not observe;while roses wince)
that which we die for lives(may never cease
views with smooth vigilant perpetual eyes
each exact victim,how he does not stir)

O love,my love!soul clings and heart conceives

and mind leaps(and that which we die for lives
as wholly as that which we live for dies)

4

a)glazed mind layed in a
                              urinal
howlessly and without why
(quite minus gal or
                         pal

slightly too sick to rightly die)
"gedup"
          the gentscoon coos
gently:tug?g(ing intently it

refuses.
          to refuse;
just,look)ing dead but not complete
-ly not(not as look men

who are turned to seem)
                          "stetti"
and
          willbeishfully bursting un-
eats wasvino isspaghett(i

5

i
(meet)t(touch)
ems crouch(
lunge
)ing bruiseD
Suddenly by thousand

starings rinsed with
thoroughly million yells they
f-oo-l(whom,blinds;blood)pa-nt
stab are

(slopped givers of not)bang
spurting mesh(faith
-ful which -ly try are ing)al

most fe(hug)males(one-t
wo-l oop-l

eftsthrowr ightsm issingupperc

uts-lurc hhurt-re
coil charge &)swooN

Crowdloomroar:ing;diskface,es
(are two
notSoft soft one are

hard one notHard)not
boys boy-
ish(a stopped A)with!notgirl'swith?dumb
(thewith girl)ness(ish The eyesthe

Is)aRe
iS ar(ise)wi
lt(wit(hprettyw)ith)mr
jeff dick
son fec

i
(m
c)
t

(m
x
x

x
ii)

I

6

exit a kind of unkindness exit

little
mr Big
notbusy
Busi
ness notman

(!ye
galleon
wilts
b:
   e;n,d

i
 ng
like like,like bad,like
candy:& you

are dead
you captain)

Memo 1
wife in impossibly
hell Memo
1 son
in improbably yale

7

sonnet entitled how to run the world)

A always don't there B being no such thing
for C can't casts no shadow D drink and

E eat of her voice in whose silence the music of spring
lives F feel opens but shuts understand
G gladly forget little having less

with every least each most remembering
H highest fly only the flag that's furled

(sestet entitled grass is flesh or swim
who can and bathe who must or any dream
means more than sleep as more than know means guess)

I item i immaculately owe
dying one life and will my rest to these

children building this rainman out of snow

8

the(
        Wistfully

dead seem generous)don't
All suspect each(nor

have i observed
some chucking some
legally into Oblivion wave little

flags weeping flatter
thoroughly imploring threaten)the
wistFully dead you directly perceive or minus
news alimony blackmail whathavewe

and propaganda(it is incredible But
others don't
scream murmur wink
at kid anæsthetize marry bump off
or otherwise amplify others)

the so to speak wistfulLy dead
are not relatively
speaking uncultured(who
Very distinctly confine

      their omnipotent literally their
      putting it more than mildly Absolute
      destructivity to non-

      entities e.
      g. the)
          whis-per it
                    (

      Living

                  9

o pr
    gress verily thou art m
    mentous superc
    lossal hyperpr
    digious etc i kn
    w & if you d

    n't why g
     to yonder s
    called newsreel s
    called theatre & with your
    wn eyes beh

    ld The
          (The president The
          president of The president
          of the The)president of

          the(united The president of the
          united states The president of the united
          states of The President Of The)United States

          Of America unde negant redire quemquam supp
sedly thr

w
  i
    n
      g
        a
       b
         aseball

1 0

little man
(in a hurry
full of an
important worry)
halt stop forget **relax**

wait

(little child
who have tried
who have failed
who have cried)
lie bravely down

sleep

big rain
big snow
big sun
big moon
(enter

us)

1 1

çi gît 1 Fœtus(unborn to not die

safely whose epoch fits him like a grave)
with all his toys(money men motors "my"
yachts wolfhounds women)and the will to shave

that Ghost is dead(whom noone might inter
fleeing himself for selves more strangely made
(wears pain at joy,come summer puts on fur

answers eats moves remembers is afraid)

each hates a Man whom both would call their friend
and who may envy neither;nor bewail
(would rather make than have and give than lend
—being through failures born who cannot fail

having no wealth but love,who shall not spend
my fortune(although endlessness should end)

1 2

why why

How many winds make wonderful
and is luck The skeleton of life
or did anybody Open a moment

are Not

more than(if Green invents because
where might Where live
can fisherMen swim and
who's myself's Antimere
Should words carry weapons)are

not Less than(that

by doDreaming heteronomously
metameric me are picked from
dumb sleePdeep
ness squirmcurl

ing homonomously metameric You

1 3

                    r-p-o-p-h-e-s-s-a-g-r
            who
a)s w(e loo)k
upnowgath
            PPEGORHRASS
                            eringint(o-
aThe):l
        eA
            !p:
S   a
            (r
rIvInG   .gRrEaPsPhOs)
                                        to
rea(be)rran(com)gi(e)ngly
,grasshopper;

14

mouse)Won
derfully is
anyone else entirely who doesn't
move(Moved more suddenly than)whose

tiniest smile?may Be
bigger than the fear of all
hearts never which have
(Per

haps)loved(or than
everyone that will Ever love)we
've
hidden him in A leaf

and,
Opening
beautiful earth
put(only)a Leaf among dark

ness.sunlight's
thenlike?now
Disappears
some

thing(silent:
madeofimagination
;the incredible soft)ness
(his ears(eyes

15

one nonsufficiently inunderstood
re
    with some difficulty
                    one father of
one(ask super-)wonderful(mother)child is a good
Husband to him(and whose what he conceives to be Love
did
    stretchandstretchandstretchandstretchand
                                 did)

who begins stuttering each sentence we both
consid
      (notb- notbr- notbre- notbrea-k
                                  . The kid)
er Santa Claus a criminal(hears Darwin;asks about **Death**)
concept

      O hairlesschested females,well
attend!list,every nonelastic male—
uplook,all joybegotten whelps whom soothe
psychotic myths like Jonah And The Whale

:oiwun uhsoi roitee runow dutmoi
jak roids wid yooze
                Vury Sin Silly
                        :oi

                1 6

        may i feel said he
        (i'll squeal said she
        just once said he)
        it's fun said she

        (may i touch said he
        how much said she
        a lot said he)
        why not said she

        (let's go said he
        not too far said she
        what's too far said he
        where you are said she)

        may i stay said he
        (which way said she
        like this said he
        if you kiss said she

        may i move said he
        is it love said she)
        if you're willing said he
        (but you're killing said she

but it's life said he
but your wife said she
now said he)
ow said she

(tiptop said he
don't stop said she
oh no said he)
go slow said she

(cccome?said he
ummm said she)
you're divine!said he
(you are Mine said she)

17

o
sure)but
nobody unders(no
but Rully yes i
know)but what it comes

to(listen you don't have to

i mean Reely)but(no listen don't
be sil why sure)i mean the(o
well ughhuh sure why not yuh course yeh well
naturally i und certain i o posi but

i know sure that's)but listen here's

(correct you said it yeah)but
listen but(it's Rilly yeh
ughhuh yuh)i know

(o sure i

know yes
of

course)but what i mean is Nobody Understands Her RERLY

18

this little
pair had a little scare
right in the middle of a bed bed
bed)when each other courted both
was very very thwarted(and
when which was aborted
what was dead dead dead)

whereupon mary
quite contrary didn't
die
(may be seen to inexactly pass and unprecisely
to repass where
flesh is heiry montparnasse
is goosed by raspail).

But he turned into a fair
y!a fair
y!!a
fair
y!!!
but she turned into a fair-y(and
it seems to be doing nicely

19

who before dying demands not rebirth

of such than hungrily more swiftness as
with(feel)pauseless immeasurably Now
cancels the childfully diminishing earth
—never whose proudly life swallowed is by

(with hope two eyes a memory this brow
five or three dreamfuls of despair that face)

large one colored nonthings of gluttonous sky—
nor(as a blind,how timidly,throb;which
hints being;suggests identity)breathes fleet
perfectly far from tangible domains
rare with most early soul
                                him shall untouch

meaningless precision and complete fate

(he must deny mind:may believe in brains.

2 0

go(perpe)go

(tu)to(al
adve

nturin
g p
article

s of s
ini
sterd
exte

ri)go to(ty)the(om
nivorou salways lugbrin
g ingseekfindlosin g
motilities
are)go to

the
ant
(al
ways

alingwaysing)
go to the ant thou go
(inging)

to the
ant,thou ant-

eater

2 1

IN)
       all those who got
       athlete's mouth jumping
       on&off bandwaggons
                              (MEMORIAM

2 2

   when muckers pimps and tratesmen
      delivered are of vicians
         and all the world howls stadesmen
         beware of politisions

         beware of folks with missians
            to turn us into rissions
            and blokes with ammunicions
            who tend to make incitions

         and pity the fool who cright
         god help me it aint no ews
      eye like the steak all ried
   but eye certainly hate the juse

2 3

   he does not have to feel because he thinks
   (the thoughts of others,be it understood)
   he does not have to think because he knows
   (that anything is bad which you think good)

   because he knows,he cannot understand
   (why Jones don't pay me what he knows he owes)
   because he cannot understand,he drinks
   (and he drinks and he drinks and he drinks and)

   not bald. (Coughs.) Two pale slippery small eyes

balanced upon one broken babypout
(pretty teeth wander into which and out
of)Life,dost Thou contain a marvel than
this death named Smith less strange?

                      Married and lies

afraid;aggressive and:American

24

"let's start a magazine

to hell with literature
we want something redblooded

lousy with pure
reeking with stark
and fearlessly obscene

but really clean
get what I mean
let's not spoil it
let's make it serious

something authentic and delirious
you know something genuine like a mark
in a toilet

graced with guts and gutted
with grace"

squeeze your nuts and open your face

25

this(that

grey)white
(man)horse

floats
on 4
3rdtoes

p
(drooli
ngly supp
ort 2 be

nt
toothpick
s)

ro
ude

stly(stuck in a spanked behind

26

what does little Ernest croon
in his death at afternoon?
(kow dow r 2 bul retoinis
wus de woids uf lil Oinis

27

little joe gould has lost his teeth and doesn't know where
to find them(and found a secondhand set which click)little
gould used to amputate his appetite with bad brittle
candy but just(nude eel)now little joe lives on air

Harvard Brevis Est for Handkerchief read Papernapkin no laundry
bills likes People preferring Negroes Indians Youse
n.b. ye twang of little joe(yankee)gould irketh sundry
who are trying to find their minds(but never had any to lose)

and a myth is as good as a smile but little joe gould's quote oral
history unquote might(publishers note)be entitled a wraith's
progress or mainly awash while chiefly submerged or an amoral
morality sort-of-aliveing by innumerable kind-of-deaths

(Amérique Je T'Aime and it may be fun to be fooled
but it's more fun to be more to be fun to be little joe gould)

28

  that famous fatheads find that each
     and every thing must have an end
  (the silly cause of trivial which
     thinkless unwishing doth depend

     upon the texture of their p-ss)
  isn't(and that it mayn't be twirled
     around your little finger is)
  what's right about the g. o. world

  what's wrong with(between me and we)
     the g--d -ld w. isn't that it
  can't exist(and is that the
     g. o. w. is full of)delete

29

  most(people

  simply

  can't)
  won't(most
  parent people mustn't

  shouldn't)most daren't

  (sortof people well
  youknow kindof)
  aint

  &

  even
  (not having
  most ever lived

                    people always)don't

                    die(becoming most
                    buried unbecomingly
                    very

                    by

                    most)people

                              3 0

          kumrads die because they're told)
          kumrads die before they're old
          (kumrads aren't afraid to die
          kumrads don't
          and kumrads won't
          believe in life)and death knows whie

          (all good kumrads you can tell
          by their altruistic smell
          moscow pipes good kumrads dance)
          kumrads enjoy
          s.freud knows whoy
          the hope that you may mess your pance

          every kumrad is a bit
          of quite unmitigated hate
          (travelling in a futile groove
          god knows why)
          and so do i
          (because they are afraid to love

                              3 1

     does yesterday's perfection seem not quite

     so clever as the pratfall of a clown
     (should stink of failure more than wars of feet

     all things whose slendering sweetness touched renown)
     suddenly themselves if all dreams unmake
     (when in a most smashed unworld stands unslain

he which knows not if any anguish struck
how thin a ghost so deep and he might live)
yes,partly nor some edgeless star could give
that anguish room;but likes it only this

eternal mere one bursting soul
                              why,then

comes peace unto men who are always men
while a man shall which a god sometimes is

I the lost shoulders S the empty spine

                        3 2

            numb(and
            that was
            and that
            was cling)

            on
            win
            ter
            sc

            ribbled
            lonely truth(from
            hang
            from droop

            w
            ar
            pin
            g dre

            ams
            whichful sarcasms
            papery deathfuls)awaits
            yes

            this alive secretly i
            frantic this serene
            mightily how rooted
            who of iron

3 3

emptied.hills.listen.
,not,alive,trees,dream(
ev:ery:wheres:ex:tend:ing:hush

)
  andDark
IshbusY
ing-roundly-dis

tinct;chuck
lings,laced
ar:e,by(

fleet&panelike&frailties
!throughwhich!brittlest!whitewhom!
f
  l o a t ?)
            r
        h y t h m s

3 4

snow)says!Says
over un
        graves
                der,speaking
(says word
Less)ly(goes

folds?folds)cold
stones(o-l-d)names
aren'ts

)L
   iv
es(c
    omeS

says)s;n;o;w(says

W
I

elds)
un
    forgetting
            un.
der(theys)the

:se!crumbs things?Its
noyesiyou
he-she
(Weres

3 5

how dark and single,where he ends,the earth
(whose texture feels of pride and loneliness
alive like some dream giving more than all
life's busy little dyings may possess)

how sincere large distinct and natural
he comes to his disappearance;as a mind
full without fear might faithfully lie down
to so much sleep they only understand

enormously which fail—look:with what ease
that bright how plural tide measures her guest
(as critics will upon a poet feast)

meanwhile this ghost goes under,his drowned girth
are mountains;and beyond all hurt of praise
the unimaginable night not known

3 6

into a truly
curving form
enters my
soul

feels all small
facts dissolved
by the lewd guess
of fabulous immensity

the sky screamed
the sun died)
the ship lifts
on seas of iron

breathing height eating
steepness the
ship climbs
murmuring silver mountains

which
disappear(and
only
was night

and through only this night a
mightily form moves
whose passenger and whose
pilot my spirit is

37

conceive a man,should he have anything
would give a little more than it away

(his autumn's winter being summer's spring
who moved by standing in november's may)
from whose(if loud most howish time derange

the silent whys of such a deathlessness)
remembrance might no patient mind unstrange
learn(nor could all earth's rotting scholars guess
that life shall not for living find the rule)

and dark beginnings are his luminous ends
who far less lonely than a fire is cool
took bedfellows for moons mountains for friends

—open your thighs to fate and(if you can
withholding nothing)World,conceive a man

SNOW

cru
   is
      ingw Hi
sperf
      ul
lydesc

BYS FLUTTERFULLY IF

(endbegi ndesginb ecend)tang
lesp
      ang
le
  s
    ofC omeg o

CRINGE WITHS

lilt(
    -ing-
         lyful
of)!
    (s
r

BIRDS BECAUSE AGAINS

emarkable
        s)h?
              y & a
                  (from n
o(into whe)re f
             ind)
nd
  ArE

GLIB SCARCELYEST AMONGS FLOWERING

39

move
deeply,rain
(dream hugely)wish
firmly. splendidly advancing colour

strike
into form
(actually)realness
kill

(make
strangely)known(establish
new)come,what
Being!open us open

our
selves. create
(suddenly announce:hurl)
blind full steep love

40

as if as

if a mys
teriouSly("i am alive"

)
 brave

ly and(th
e moon's al-down)most whis
per(here)ingc r O

wing;ly:cry.be,gi N s agAins

t b
ecomin
gsky?t r e e s
!

m ore&(o uto f)mor e torn(f og r
e
elingwhiRls)are pouring rush fields drea
mf(ull
        y
          are.)
&
som
ewhereishbudofshape

now,s
tI
r
ghost

?s

tirf lic;k
e rsM-o
:ke(c.
        l

i,

m
  !
b
) & it:s;elf,

mmamakmakemakesWwOwoRworLworlD

4 1

here's to opening and upward,to leaf and to sap
and to your(in my arms flowering so new)
self whose eyes smell of the sound of rain

and here's to silent certainly mountains;and to
a disappearing poet of always,snow
and to morning;and to morning's beautiful friend
twilight(and a first dream called ocean)and

let must or if be damned with whomever's afraid
down with ought with because with every brain
which thinks it thinks,nor dares to feel(but up
with joy;and up with laughing and drunkenness)

here's to one undiscoverable guess
of whose mad skill each world of blood is made
(whose fatal songs are moving in the moon

42

out of a supermetamathical subpreincestures
pooped universe(of croons canned
à la vallee and preserved goldfishian gestures)
suddenly sally rand

handsomely who did because she could what the movies try
to do because they can't i mean move
yes sir she jes was which the radio aint(proov
-ing that the quickness of the fand intrigues the fly)

for know all men(χαίρετε)
as it was in the beginning it(rejoice)
was and ever shall be nor every partialness beats one entirety
neither may shadow down flesh neither may vibration create voice

if therefore among foul pains appears an if emerges a joy let
's thank indecent
god p.s. the most successful b.o.fully speaking concession at the recent
world's fair was the paytoilet

43

theys sO alive
              (who is
                    ?niggers)

            Not jes
            livin
            not Jes alive But
            So alive(they

        s
        born alive)
        some folks aint born
        somes born dead an
        somes born alive(but

      niggers
       is
      all
     born
    so
  Alive)

        ump-A-tum
                ;tee-die

        uM-tuM
                tidl
                  -id

        umptyumpty(OO——

                                !
            ting
        Bam-
      :do)
  ,chippity.

44*

* *In holograph edition only*

45

sometimes
     in)Spring a someone will lie(glued
among familiar things newly which are
transferred with dusk)wondering why this star
does not fall into his mind
        feeling
throughout ignorant disappearing me
hurling vastness of love(sometimes in Spring
somewhere between what is and what may be
unknown most secret i will breathe such crude
perfection as divides by timelessness
that heartbeat)
      mightily forgetting all
which will forget him(emptying our soul
of emptiness)priming at every pore
a deathless life with magic until peace
outthunders silence.
      And(night climbs the air

46

swi(
   across!gold's

rouNdly
)ftblac
kl(ness)y

a-motion-upo-nmotio-n

Less?
   thE
(against
is
)Swi

mming

(w-a)s
bIr

d,

47

ondumonde"

(first than caref
ully;pois
edN-o wt he
n
,whysprig
          sli

nkil
-Y-
strol(pre)ling(cise)dy(ly)na(
mite)

   :yearnswoons;

    &Isdensekil-
    ling-whipAlert-floatScor
    ruptingly)

                ça-y-est
                droppe5
                 qu'est-ce que tu veux
                Dwrith
                 il est trop fort le nègre
                esn7othingish8s
                c'est fini
                pRaW,lT;O:
                allons
            9
          &
          .

                (musically-who?

     pivoting)
     SmileS

        "ahlbrhoon

4 8

floatfloafloflf
lloloa
tatoatloatf loat fl oat
f loatI ngL

y

&fris
klispin
glyT
　　w
　　　irlErec

，

t,
;d
;:a:
nC.eda:Nci;ddaanncciinn

(GlY)

a
　nda
　　　n-saint
dance!Dan
Sai ntd anc

&e&

—cupidoergosum
spun=flash
omiepsicronlonO—
megaeta?
　　　　P
　　　aul D-as-in-tip-toe r

apeR

49

silent unday by silently not night

did the great world(in darkly taking rain)
drown,beyond sound
                        down(slowly
                                  beneath
                                              sight
fall
   ing)fall
            ing through touch
                            less stillness(seized

among what ghostly nevers of again)
silent not night by silently unday
life's bright less dwindled to a leastful most
under imagination. When(out of sheer

nothing)came a huger than fear a

white with madness wind and broke oceans and tore
mountains from their sockets and strewed the black air
with writhing alive skies—and in death's place
new fragrantly young earth space opening was.
Were your eyes:lost,believing;hushed with when

5 0

     much i cannot)
     tear up the world:& toss
     it away;or
     cause one causeless cloud to purely grow

     but,never
     doubt my weakness
     makes more than most
     strength(less than these how

less than least flowers of rain)thickly
i fail slenderly i
win(like touch all stars or
to live in the moon

a while)and shall
carve time so we'll before
what's death
come(in one bed.

5 1

at dusk
           just when
the Light is filled with birds
seriously
i begin

to climb the best hill,
driven by black wine.
a village does not move behind
my eye

the windmills are
silent
their flattened arms
complain steadily against the west

one Clock dimly cries
nine,i stride among the vines
(my heart pursues
against the little moon

a here and there lark
                          who;rises,
and;droops
as if upon a thread invisible)

A graveyard dreams through its
cluttered and brittle emblems,or
a field(and i pause among
the smell of minute mown lives)oh

my spirit you
tumble
climb
     and mightily fatally

i remark how through deep lifted
fields Oxen distinctly move,a
yellowandbluish cat(perched why
Curvingly at this)window;yes

women sturdily meander in my
mind,woven by always upon
sunset,
crickets within me whisper

whose erect blood finally
trembles,emerging to perceive
buried in cliff
        precisely

at the Ending of this road,
a candle in a shrine:
its puniest flame persists
shaken by the sea

52

Spring(side

walks are)is
most(windows where blaze

naLOVEme
crazily
ships

bulge hearts by
darts pierced lazily writhe
lurch faceflowers stutter
treebodies wobbly-

ing thing
-birds)sing-
u
(cities are houses
people are flies who

buzz on)-lar(windows called sidewalks
of houses called cities)spring
most singular-
ly(cities are houses are)is(are owned

by a m- by
a -n by a
-oo-

is old as
the jews are a moon is

as round as)Death

53

what a proud dreamhorse pulling(smoothloomingly)through
(stepp)this(ing)crazily seething of this
raving city screamingly street wonderful

flowers And o the Light thrown by Them opens

sharp holes in dark places paints eyes touches hands with newness and these startled whats are a(piercing clothes thoughts kiss
-ing wishes bodies)squirm-of-frightened shy are whichs small
its hungry for Is for Love Spring thirsty for happens
only and beautiful
                    there is a ragged beside the who limps
man crying silence upward
                              —to have tasted Beautiful to have known
Only to have smelled Happens—skip dance kids hop point at
red blue yellow violet white orange green-
ness

    o what a proud dreamhorse moving(whose feet
almost walk air). now who stops. Smiles.he
                                        stamps

54

Jehovah buried,Satan dead,
do fearers worship Much and Quick;
badness not being felt as bad,
itself thinks goodness what is meek;
obey says toc,submit says tic,
Eternity's a Five Year Plan:
if Joy with Pain shall hang in hock
who dares to call himself a man?

go dreamless knaves on Shadows fed,
your Harry's Tom,your Tom is Dick;
while Gadgets murder squawk and add,
the cult of Same is all the chic;
by instruments,both span and spic,
are justly measured Spic and Span:
to kiss the mike if Jew turn kike
who dares to call himself a man?

loudly for Truth have liars pled,
their heels for Freedom slaves will click;
where Boobs are holy,poets mad,
illustrious punks of Progress shriek;
when Souls are outlawed,Hearts are sick,
Hearts being sick,Minds nothing can:
if Hate's a game and Love's a φυκ
who dares to call himself a man?

King Christ,this world is all aleak;
and lifepreservers there are none:
and waves which only He may walk
Who dares to call Himself a man.

55

worshipping Same
they squirm and they spawn
and a world is for them,them;whose
death's to be born)

his birth is their fear is their blind fear
—haunts all unsleep
this cry of one fiend,
a thousand dreams thick

(cringing they brood
breeding they wince)
his laugh is a million griefs wide(it
shall bury much stench)

and a hundred joys high are such shoulders
as cowards will scheme
to harness:let all
unfools of unbeing

set traps for his heart,
lay snares for his feet
(who wanders through only white darkness
who moves in black light

dancing isn'ts on why,digging bridges with mirrors
from whispers to stars;
climbing silence for ifs
diving under because)

only who'll say
"and this be my fame,
the harder the wind blows the
taller i am"

56

this mind made war
being generous
this heart could dare)
unhearts can less

unminds must fear
because and why
what filth is here
unlives do cry

on him they shat
they shat encore
he laughed and spat
(this life could dare

freely to give
as gives a friend
not those who slave
unselves to lend

for hope of hope
must coo or boo
may strut or creep
ungenerous who

ape deftly aims
they dare not share)
such make their names
(this poet made war

whose naught and all
sun are and moon
come fair come foul
he goes alone

daring to dare
for joy of joy)
what stink is here
unpoets do cry

unfools unfree
undeaths who live
nor shall they be
and must they have

at him they fart
they fart full oft
(with mind with heart
he spat and laughed

with self with life
this poet arose
nor hate nor grief
can go where goes

this whyless soul
a loneliest road
who dares to stroll
almost this god

this surely dream
perhaps this ghost)
humbly and whom
for worst or best

(and proudly things
only which grow
and the rain's wings
the birds of snow

things without name
beyond because
things over blame
things under praise

glad things or free
truly which live
always shall be
may never have)

do i salute
(by moon by sun
i deeply greet
this fool and man

57

when
        from a sidewalk
                        out of(blown never quite to
-gether by large sorry)creatures out
of(clumsily shining out of)instru-
ments,waltzing;undigestibly:groans.bounce

!o-ras-ourh an-dorg-an ble-at-ssw-ee-t-noth ings orarancidhurd
ygurdygur glingth umpssomet hings(whi,le sp,arrow,s wince
among those skeletons of these trees)
                                        when
                                                sunbeams loot
furnished rooms through whose foul windows absurd
clouds cruise nobly ridiculous skies

(the;mselve;s a;nd scr;a;tch-ing lousy full.of.rain
beggars yaw:nstretchy:awn)
                              then,
                                    o my love
                                                ,then
it's Spring
          immortal Always & lewd shy New

and upon the beyond imagining spasm rise
we
    you-with-me
              around(me)you
                            IYou

                              5 8

          love is a place
          & through this place of
          love move
          (with brightness of peace)
          all places

          yes is a world
          & in this world of
          yes live
          (skilfully curled)
          all worlds

                              5 9

        (b
      eLl
          s?
              bE

-ginningly)come-swarm:faces
ar;rive go.faces a(live)
sob bel
ls

(pour wo
      (things)
            men
               selves-them

inghurl)bangbells(yawnchurches
suck people)reel(dark-
ly)whirling
in

(b
  ellSB
      el
        Ls)

-to sun(crash). Streets
glit
ter
a,strut:do;colours;are:m,ove

o im
    -pos-
        sibl
          y

(ShoutflowereD
flowerish boom
b el Lsb El l
s!cry)

(be
  llsbe
    lls)
        b
           (be
              llsbell)
                  ells
                      (sbells)

sh estiffl
ystrut sal
lif san
dbut sth

epoutin(gWh.ono:w
s li psh ergo
wnd ow n,
                 r
Eve

aling 2 a
-sprout eyelands)sin
uously&them&twi
tching,begins

unununun?
butbutbut??
tonton???
ing????

—Out-&
        steps;which
flipchucking
.grins
gRiNdS

d is app ea r in gly
eyes grip live loop croon mime
nakedly hurl asquirm the
dip&giveswoop&swoon&ingly

seethe firm swirl hips whirling climb to
GIVE
(yoursmine mineyours yoursmine
!
i( )t)

61

love's function is to fabricate unknownness

(known being wishless;but love,all of wishing)
though life's lived wrongsideout,sameness chokes oneness
truth is confused with fact,fish boast of fishing

and men are caught by worms(love may not care
if time totters,light droops,all measures bend
nor marvel if a thought should weigh a star
—dreads dying least;and less,that death should end)

how lucky lovers are(whose selves abide
under whatever shall discovered be)
whose ignorant each breathing dares to hide
more than most fabulous wisdom fears to see

(who laugh and cry)who dream,create and kill
while the whole moves;and every part stands still:

62

we)under)over,the thing of floating Of
;elate
shyly a-live keen parallel specks float-ing create
height,
       liv-

ing
   ly who:seemSwoop
                  (whir
-ling be,yond!thought
are.more(Than girl

's
tears boy Dream's)forge

tful:e
     ver than,is e
           ven:th
               e(s
                  e
               a's;m
                  e,
                    m(or.y

322

                63
            birds(
                here,inven
            ting air
            U
)sing
                tw
            iligH(
            t's
                v
                va
                    vas(
            vast

            ness.Be)look
            now
                (come
            soul;
            &:and

            who
                s)e
                    voi
            c
            es
            (
              are
                ar
                  a

                64
    Do.
    omful
    relaxing

    -ly)i
    downrise outwrithein-
    ing upfall and

Am the glad deep the living from nowh
-ere(!firm!)exp-
anding,am a fe

-rvently(susta-
inin
-gness Am

root air rock day)
:you;
smile,hands

(an-
onymo
-Us

65

if night's mostness(and whom did merely day
close)
    opens
       if more than silence silent are more
flowering than stars whitely births of mind

if air is throbbing prayers whom kneeling eyes
(until perfectly their imperfect gaze
climbs this steep fragrance of eternity)
world by than worlds immenser world will pray

so(unlove disappearing)only your
less than guessed more than beauty begins the
most not imagined life adventuring
who would feel if spring's least breathing should cause
a colour
    and i do not know him
         (and

while behind death's death whenless voices sing
everywhere your selves himself recognize)

66

death(having lost)put on his universe
and yawned:it looks like rain
(they've played for timelessness
with chips of when)
that's yours;i guess
you'll have to loan me pain
to take the hearse,
see you again.

Love(having found)wound up such pretty toys
as themselves could not know:
the earth tinily whirls;
while daisies grow
(and boys and girls
have whispered thus and so)
and girls with boys
to bed will go,

67

come(all you mischief-
hatchers hatch
mischief)all you

guilty
scamper(you bastards throw dynamite)
let knowings magic
with bright credos each divisible fool

(life imitate gossip fear unlife
mean
-ness,and
to succeed in not
dying)

Is will still occur;birds disappear
becomingly:a thunderbolt compose poems
not because harm symmetry
earthquakes starfish(but
because nobody
can sell the Moon to The)moon

68

be of love(a little)
More careful
Than of everything
guard her perhaps only

A trifle less
(merely beyond how very)
closely than
Nothing,remember love by frequent

anguish(imagine
Her least never with most
memory)give entirely each
Forever its freedom

(Dare until a flower,
understanding sizelessly sunlight
Open what thousandth why and
discover laughing)

69

reason let others give and realness bring—
ask the always impossible of me
and shall who wave among your deepening
thighs a greedier wand than even death's

what beneath breathing selves transported are
into how suddenly so huge a home
(only more than immeasurable dream
wherelessly spiralling)beyond time's sky

and through this opening universe will wraiths
of doom rush(which all ghosts of life became)
and does our fatally unshadowing fate
put on one not imaginable star

:then a small million of dark voices sing
against the awful mystery of light

brIght

bRight s??? big
(soft)

soft near calm
(Bright)
calm st?? holy

(soft briGht deep)
yeS near sta? calm star big yEs
alone
(wHo

Yes
near deep whO big alone soft near
deep calm deep
????Ht ?????T)
Who(holy alone)holy(alone holy)alone

7 1

morsel miraculous and meaningless

secret on luminous whose selves and lives
imperishably feast all timeless souls

(the not whose spiral hunger may appease
what merely riches of our pretty world
sweetly who flourishes,swiftly which fails

but out of serene perfectly Nothing hurled
into young Now entirely arrives
gesture past fragrance fragrant;a than pure

more signalling of singular most flame
and surely poets only understands)
honour this loneliness of even him

who fears and eyes lifts lifting hopes and hands
—nourish my failure with thy freedom:star

isful beckoningly fabulous crumb

AND
THANKS
TO
R. H. C.

New Poems

[from COLLECTED POEMS]

INTRODUCTION

The poems to come are for you and for me and are not for mostpeople
—it's no use trying to pretend that mostpeople and ourselves are alike.
Mostpeople have less in common with ourselves than the squarerootof-
minusone. You and I are human beings;mostpeople are snobs.

Take the matter of being born. What does being born mean to mostpeople? Catastrophe unmitigated. Socialrevolution. The cultured aristo-
crat yanked out of his hyperexclusively ultravoluptuous superpalazzo,and
dumped into an incredibly vulgar detentioncamp swarming with every
conceivable species of undesirable organism. Mostpeople fancy a guaran-
teed birthproof safetysuit of nondestructible selflessness. If mostpeople
were to be born twice they'd improbably call it dying—

you and I are not snobs. We can never be born enough. We are human
beings;for whom birth is a supremely welcome mystery,the mystery of
growing:the mystery which happens only and whenever we are faithful
to ourselves. You and I wear the dangerous looseness of doom and find it
becoming. Life,for eternal us,is now;and now is much too busy being
a little more than everything to seem anything,catastrophic included.

Life,for mostpeople,simply isn't. Take the socalled standardofliving.
What do mostpeople mean by "living"? They don't mean living. They
mean the latest and closest plural approximation to singular prenatal
passivity which science,in its finite but unbounded wisdom,has succeeded
in selling their wives. If science could fail,a mountain's a mammal. Mostpeople's wives can spot a genuine delusion of embryonic omnipotence
immediately and will accept no substitutes

—luckily for us,a mountain is a mammal. The plusorminus movie to end
moving,the strictly scientific parlourgame of real unreality,the tyranny
conceived in misconception and dedicated to the proposition that every
man is a woman and any woman a king,hasn't a wheel to stand on. What
their most synthetic not to mention transparent majesty,mrsandmr collective foetus,would improbably call a ghost is walking. He isn't an undream of anaesthetized impersons,or a cosmic comfortstation,or a tran-
scendentally sterilized lookiesoundiefeelietastiesmellie. He is a healthily
complex,a naturally homogeneous,citizen of immortality. The now of his
each pitying free imperfect gesture,his any birth or breathing,insults per-

331

fected inframortally millenniums of slavishness. He is a little more than everything,he is democracy;he is alive:he is ourselves.

Miracles are to come. With you I leave a remembrance of miracles: they are by somebody who can love and who shall be continually reborn, a human being;somebody who said to those near him,when his fingers would not hold a brush "tie it into my hand"—

nothing proving or sick or partial. Nothing false,nothing difficult or easy or small or colossal. Nothing ordinary or extraordinary,nothing emptied or filled,real or unreal;nothing feeble and known or clumsy and guessed. Everywhere tints childrening,innocent spontaneous,true. Nowhere possibly what flesh and impossibly such a garden,but actually flowers which breasts are among the very mouths of light. Nothing believed or doubted;brain over heart, surface:nowhere hating or to fear; shadow,mind without soul. Only how measureless cool flames of making; only each other building always distinct selves of mutual entirely opening; only alive. Never the murdered finalities of wherewhen and yesno,impotent nongames of wrongright and rightwrong;never to gain or pause,never the soft adventure of undoom,greedy anguishes and cringing ecstasies of inexistence;never to rest and never to have:only to grow.

Always the beautiful answer who asks a more beautiful question

E. E. CUMMINGS

1

un
der fog
's
touch

slo

ings
fin
gering
s

wli

whichs
turn
in
to whos

est

people
be
come
un

2

kind)
YM&WC
(of sort of)
A soursweet bedtime

-less un-
(wonderful)
story atrickling a
-rithmetic o-

ver me you & all those & that
"I may say professor"
asleep
wop "shapley

has compared the universe
to a
uh" pause
"Cookie

but" nonvisibly smi-
ling through man
-ufactured harmlessly accurate
gloom "I

think he might now be inclined to describe
it rather as
a" pause "uh"
cough

"Biscuit"
(& so on & so unto canned
swoonsong
came "I wish you good" the mechanical

dawn
"morning")& that those you
i St
ep

into the not
merely immeasurable into
the mightily alive the
dear beautiful eternal night

                              3

a football with white eyebrows the
3
rd chief something or must be off

duty wanderfuling aft spits)
int
o immensity(upon once whom

fiercely by pink mr seized green
mrs
opening is it horribly smith spouts

cornucopiously not unrecognizable whats of
t
oo vertiginously absorbed which à la

4

(of Ever-Ever Land i speak
sweet morons gather roun'
who does not dare to stand or sit
may take it lying down)

down with the human soul
and anything else uncanned
for everyone carries canopeners
in Ever-Ever Land

(for Ever-Ever Land is a place
that's as simple as simple can be
and was built that way on purpose
by simple people like we)

down with hell and heaven
and all the religious fuss
infinity pleased our parents
one inch looks good to us

(and Ever-Ever Land is a place
that's measured and safe and known
where it's lucky to be unlucky
and the hitler lies down with the cohn)

down above all with love
and everything perverse
or which makes some feel more better
when all ought to feel less worse

(but only sameness is normal
in Ever-Ever Land
for a bad cigar is a woman
but a gland is only a gland)

5

lucky means finding
Holes where
pockets aren't lucky
's to spend

laughter
not money lucky are
Breathe
grow dream

die love not
Fear eat sleep kill
and have you am luck
-y is we lucky luck-

ier
luck
-I-
est

6

Q:dwo
   we know of anything which can
   be as dull as one englishman
A:to

7

&-moon-He-be-hind-a-mills

tosses like thin bums dream
ing i'm thick in a hot young queen with

a twot with a twitch like kingdom
come(moon
The

sq
uirmwri
th-ing out of wonderful
thunder!of?ocean.a

ndn
ooneandfor
e-ver)moon She over this new eng
land fragrance of pasture and now ti

p toe ingt o
a child who alone st
and

s(not a
fraid of moon You)

not-mere-ly-won-der-ing-&

                    8

    this little bride & groom are
    standing)in a kind
    of crown he dressed
    in black candy she

    veiled with candy white
    carrying a bouquet of
    pretend flowers this
    candy crown with this candy

    little bride & little
    groom in it kind of stands on
    a thin ring which stands on a much
    less thin very much more

    big & kinder of ring & which
    kinder of stands on a
    much more than very much
    biggest & thickest & kindest

    of ring & all one two three rings
    are cake & everything is protected by
    cellophane against anything(because
    nothing really exists

9

so little he is
so.
     Little
ness be

(ing)
comes ex
-pert-
Ly expand:grO

  w
    i
?n
    g

Is poet iS
(childlost
so;ul
)foundclown a

-live a
,bird
!O
& j &

ji
&
jim,jimm
;jimmy

s:
    A
   V
  o(

10

nor woman
                (just as it be

        gan to snow he dis
            a

                ppeare
                    d leavi
                        ng on its

                    elf pro
                        pped uprigh
                            t that in this o
                        ther w

                    ise how e
                        mpty park bundl
                        e of what man can

                't hurt any more h
                    u
                sh
nor child)

11

my specialty is living said
a man(who could not earn his bread
because he would not sell his head)

squads right impatiently replied
two billion pubic lice inside
one pair of trousers(which had died)

12

The Mind's(

i never you never
he she or it

never we you and they never
saw so
much heard so much smelled so much

tasted
plus touched quite so And
How much nonexistence
eye sed bea

yew tea mis
eyesucks unyewkuntel finglestein idstings
yewrety oride lesgo eckshun

kemeruh daretoi
nig

)Ah,Soul

13

if i

or anybody don't
know where it her his

my next meal's coming from
i say to hell with that
that doesn't matter(and if

he she it or everybody gets a
bellyful without
lifting my finger i say to hell
with that i

say that doesn't matter)but
if somebody
or you are beautiful or
deep or generous what
i say is

whistle that
sing that yell that spell
that out big(bigger than cosmic
rays war earthquakes famine or the ex

prince of whoses diving into
a whatses to rescue miss nobody's
probably handbag)because i say that's not

swell(get me)babe not(understand me)lousy
kid that's something else my sweet(i feel that's

true)

14

hanged

if n
y in a real hot spell
with o

man

what bubbies going
places on such
babies aint plenty
good enough for

i

eu
can have
you

rope

15

economic secu
rity" is a cu
rious excu

se
(in

use among pu
rposive pu
nks)for pu

tting the arse
before the torse

16

beware beware beware
because because because
equals(transparent or

science must
bait laws with
stars to catch telescopes

)why.
Being is
patience is patient is(patiently

all the eyes of these with listening
hands only fishermen are
prevented by cathedrals

17

only as what(out of a flophouse)floats
on murdered feet into immense no

Where
        which to map while these not eyes quite try
almost their mind immeasurably roots
among much soundless rubbish of guitars
and watches
        only as this(which might have been
a man and kept a date and played a tune)
death's dollhead wandering under weakening stars

Feels;if
        & god said & there was
                                is born:
one face who.
                and hands hold his whose unlife
bursts

        only so;only if you should turn
the infinite corner of love,all that i am
easily disappears(leaving no proof

not the least shadow of a. Not one smallest dream)

1 8

must being shall

one only thing must:the opening of a
(not some not every but any)
heart—wholly,idiotically—before
such nonsense which
is the overlove & underwish of
beauty;before keen if
dim quiveringly
spangle & thingless
& before flashing soft neverwheres &
sweet nothingly gushing tinsel;silently
yes before angel curvings upon a mostless
more of star

o-

pening of(writhing your exploding my)heart
before how worlds delicate
of bombast—papery what
& vast solidities,unwinding
dizzily &
mirrors;sprung dimensionless
new alls of joy:quietly & before illimitably
spiralling candy of tiniest
forever—crazily from totally sprouted by alive
green each very lifting
& seriously voice
-like finger of

the tree

1 9

may my heart always be open to little
birds who are the secrets of living
whatever they sing is better than to know
and if men should not hear them men are old

may my mind stroll about hungry
and fearless and thirsty and supple
and even if it's sunday may i be wrong
for whenever men are right they are not young

and may myself do nothing usefully
and love yourself so more than truly
there's never been quite such a fool who could fail
pulling all the sky over him with one smile

20

the people who
rain(are move as)proces
-sion Its oflike immens-
ely(a feet which is prayer

among)float withins he
upclimbest And(sky she
)open new(
dark we all findingly Spring the

Fragrance unvisible)ges
-tured together-
ly singing ams
trample(they flyingly silence

21

porky & porkie
sit into a moon)

blacker than dreams
are round like a spoon are
both making silence

two-made-of-one

& nothing tells anywhere
"snow will come soon" &
pretending they're birds sit

creatures of quills
(asleep who must go

things-without-wings

22

you shall above all things be glad and young.
For if you're young,whatever life you wear

it will become you;and if you are glad
whatever's living will yourself become.
Girlboys may nothing more than boygirls need:
i can entirely her only love

whose any mystery makes every man's
flesh put space on;and his mind take off time

that you should ever think,may god forbid
and(in his mercy)your true lover spare:
for that way knowledge lies,the foetal grave
called progress,and negation's dead undoom.

I'd rather learn from one bird how to sing
than teach ten thousand stars how not to dance

50 Poems

to m. m.

1

!blac
k
agains
t

(whi)

te sky
?t
rees whic
h fr

om droppe

d

,
le
af

a:;go

e
s wh
IrlI
n

·g

2

fl

a
tt
ene

d d

reaml
essn
esse

s wa

it
sp
i

t)(t

he
s
e

f

ooli
sh sh
apes

ccocoucougcoughcoughi

ng with me
n more o
n than in the

m

3

If you can't eat you got to

smoke and we aint got
nothing to smoke:come on kid

let's go to sleep
if you can't smoke you got to

Sing and we aint got

nothing to sing;come on kid
let's go to sleep

if you can't sing you got to
die and we aint got

Nothing to die,come on kid

let's go to sleep
if you can't die you got to

dream and we aint got
nothing to dream(come on kid

Let's go to sleep)

4

nobody loved this
he)with its
of eye stuck
into a rock of

forehead.No
body

loved
big that quick
sharp
thick snake of a

voice these

root
like legs
or
feethands;

nobody
ever could ever

had love loved whose his
climbing shoulders queerly twilight
:never,no
(body.

Nothing

5

am was. are leaves few this. is these a or
scratchily over which of earth dragged once
-ful leaf. & were who skies clutch an of poor
how colding hereless. air theres what immense
live without every dancing. singless only a child's eyes float silently down
more than two those that and that noing our
gone snow gone
                    yours mine
                          . We're
alive and shall be:cities may overflow(am
was)assassinating whole grassblades,five
ideas can swallow a man;three words im
-prison a woman for all her now:but we've
such freedom such intense digestion so
much greenness only dying makes us grow

6

flotsam and jetsam
are gentlemen poeds
urseappeal netsam
our spinsters and coeds)

thoroughly bretish
they scout the inhuman
itarian fetish
that man isn't wuman

vive the millenni
um three cheers for labor
give all things to enni
one bugger thy nabor

(neck and senecktie
are gentlemen ppoyds
even whose recktie
are covered by lloyd's

7

moan
(is)
ing

the she of the
sea
un

der a who
a he a moon a
magic out

of the black this which of
one street leaps quick
squirmthicklying lu

minous night
mare som
e w

hereanynoevery
ing(danc)ing
wills&weres

8

the Noster was a ship of swank
(as gallant as they come)
until she hit a mine and sank
just off the coast of Sum

precisely where a craft of cost
the Ergo perished later
all hands(you may recall)being lost
including captain Pater

9

warped this perhapsy
stumbl
i
 NgflounderpirouettiN

                        g

:seized(

tatterdemalion
dow
     nupfloatsw
            oon
InG

s ly)tuck.s its(ghostsoul sheshape)

elf into leasting forever most
magical maybes of certainly
never the iswas

teetertiptotterish

sp-
   inwhirlpin
              -wh
EEling
;a!who,

(

whic hbubble ssomethin
gabou tlov
e)

10

spoke joe to jack

leave heɪ alone
she's not your gal

jack spoke to joe
's left crashed
pal dropped

o god alice
yells but who shot
up grabbing had
by my throat me

give it him good
a bottle she
quick who stop damned
fall all we go spill

and chairs tables the and
bitch whispers jill
mopping too bad

dear sh not yet
jesus what blood

darling i said

11

red-rag and pink-flag
blackshirt and brown
strut-mince and stink-brag
have all come to town

some like it shot
and some like it hung
and some like it in the twot
nine months young

1 2

(will you teach a
wretch to live
straighter than a needle)

ask
    her
        ask
            when
                (ask and
                ask
                and ask
again and)ask a
brittle little
person fiddling
in
the
rain

(did you kiss
a girl with nipples
like pink thimbles)

ask
    him
        ask
            who
                (ask and
                ask
                and ask
ago and)ask a
simple
crazy
thing
singing
in the snow

13

proud of his scientific attitude

and liked the prince of wales wife wants to die
but the doctors won't let her comma considers frood
whom he pronounces young mistaken and
cradles in rubbery one somewhat hand
the paper destinies of nations sic
item a bounceless period unshy
the empty house is full O Yes of guk
rooms daughter item son a woopsing queer
colon hobby photography never has plumbed
the heights of prowst but respects artists if
they are sincere proud of his scientif
ic attitude and liked the king of)hear

ye!the godless are the dull and the dull are the damned

14

the way to hump a cow is not
to get yourself a stool
but draw a line around the spot
and call it beautifool

to multiply because and why
dividing thens by nows
and adding and(i understand)
is hows to hump a cows

the way to hump a cow is not
to elevate your tool
but drop a penny in the slot
and bellow like a bool

to lay a wreath from ancient greath
on insulated brows
(while tossing boms at uncle toms)
is hows to hump a cows

the way to hump a cow is not
to push and then to pull
but practicing the art of swot
to preach the golden rull

to vote for me(all decent mem
and wonens will allows
which if they don't to hell with them)
is hows to hump a cows

15

mrs

& mr across the way are kind of
afraid)afraid

of what(of

a crazy man)don't
ask me how i know(a he of head
comes to some dirty window every)twilight i

feel(his lousy eyes roaming)wonderful all

sky(a little mouth)stumbling(can't
keep up with how big very
them)now(it tears
off rag its

of

mind chucks away flimsy
which but)always(they're
more much further off)further these
those three disappear finally what's left

behind is(just a head of he

is)merely(a pair of ears with some
lips plus a couple of)holes probably that's what
(mr & mrs are

sort of really

really kind
of afraid of)these(down pull & who'll

shades

16

)when what hugs stopping earth than silent is
more silent than more than much more is or
total sun oceaning than any this
tear jumping from each most least eye of star

and without was if minus and shall be
immeasurable happenless unnow
shuts more than open could that every tree
or than all life more death begins to grow

end's ending then these dolls of joy and grief
these recent memories of future dream
these perhaps who have lost their shadows if
which did not do the losing spectres mime

until out of merely not nothing comes
only one snowflake(and we speak our names

17

youful

larger
of smallish)

Humble a
rosily
,nimblest;

c-urlin-g
noworld
Silent is

blue
(sleep!new

girlgold

1 8

ecco a letter starting "dearest we"
unsigned:remarkably brief but covering
one complete miracle of nearest far

"i cordially invite me to become
noone except yourselves r s v p"

she cannot read or write,la moon. Employs
a very crazily how clownlike that
this quickly ghost scribbling from there to where

—name unless i'm mistaken chauvesouris—
whose grammar is atrocious;but so what

princess selene doesn't know a thing
who's much too busy being her beautiful yes.
The place is now
                          let us accept
                                    (the time

forever,and you'll wear your silver shoes

1 9

there is a here and

that here was a
town(and the town is

so aged the ocean
wanders the streets are so
ancient the houses enter the

people are so feeble the feeble go to
sleep if the people sit down)
and this light is so dark the mountains
grow up from

the sky is so near the earth does not
open her
eyes(but the
feeble are people the feeble
are so wise the people

remember being born)
when and
if nothing disappears they
will disappear always who are filled

with never are more than
more is are mostly
almost are feebler than feeble are

fable who are less than these are least is who
are am(beyond when behind where under

un)

2 0

harder perhaps than a newengland bed

these ends of arms which pinch that purple book
between what hands had been before they died

squirming:now withered and unself her gnarled
vomits a rock of mindscream into life;
possibly darker than a spinster's heart

my voice feels who inquires is your cough
better today?nn-nn went head face goes

(if how begins a pillow's green means face

or why a quilt's pink stops might equal head).
Then with the splendor of an angel's fart

came one trembling out of huge each eye look
"thank you" nicely the lady's small grin said
(with more simplicity than makes a world)

2 1

six

are in a room's dark around)
five

(are all dancesing singdance all are

three
with faces made of cloud dancing and
three
singing with voices made of earth and

six are in a room's dark around)

five
(six are in a room's)
one

is red

and(six are in)
four are

white

(three singdance six dancesing three
all around around all
clouds singing three and
and three dancing earths

three menandwomen three

and all around all and
all around five all
around five around)

five flowers five

(six are in a room's dark)
all five are one

flowers five flowers and all one is fire

22

nouns to nouns

wan
wan

too nons too

and
and

nuns two nuns

w an d
ering

in sin

g
ular untheknowndulous **s**

pring

23

a pretty a day
(and every fades)
is here and away
(but born are maids
to flower an hour
in all,all)

o yes to flower
until so blithe
a doer a wooer
some limber and lithe
some very fine mower
a tall;tall

some jerry so very
(and nellie and fan)
some handsomest harry
(and sally and nan
they tremble and cower
so pale:pale)

for betty was born
to never say nay
but lucy could learn
and lily could pray
and fewer were shyer
than doll.   doll

24

these people socalled were not given hearts
how should they be?their socalled hearts would think
these socalled people have no minds but if
they had their minds socalled would not exist

but if these not existing minds took life
such life could not begin to live id est
breathe but if such life could its breath would stink

and as for souls why souls are wholes not parts
but all these hundreds upon thousands of
people socalled if multiplied by twice
infinity could never equal one)

which may your million selves and my suffice
to through the only mystery of love
become while every sun goes round its moon

25

as freedom is a breakfastfood
or truth can live with right and wrong
or molehills are from mountains made
—long enough and just so long
will being pay the rent of seem
and genius please the talentgang
and water most encourage flame

as hatracks into peachtrees grow
or hopes dance best on bald men's hair
and every finger is a toe
and any courage is a fear
—long enough and just so long
will the impure think all things pure
and hornets wail by children stung

or as the seeing are the blind
and robins never welcome spring
nor flatfolk prove their world is round
nor dingsters die at break of dong
and common's rare and millstones float
—long enough and just so long
tomorrow will not be too late

worms are the words but joy's the voice
down shall go which and up come who
breasts will be breasts thighs will be thighs
deeds cannot dream what dreams can do
—time is a tree(this life one leaf)
but love is the sky and i am for you
just so long and long enough

26

wherelings whenlings
(daughters of ifbut offspring of hopefear
sons of unless and children of almost)
never shall guess the dimension of

him whose
each
foot likes the
here of this earth

whose both
eyes
love
this now of the sky

—endlings of isn't
shall never
begin
to begin to

imagine how(only are shall be were
dawn dark rain snow rain
-bow &
a

moon
's whis-
per
in sunset

or thrushes toward dusk among whippoorwills or
tree field rock hollyhock forest brook chickadee
mountain. Mountain)
whycoloured worlds of because do

not stand against yes which is built by
forever & sunsmell
(sometimes a wonder
of wild roses

sometimes)
with north
over
the barn

27

buy me an ounce and i'll sell you a pound.
Turn
gert
      (spin!
helen)the
slimmer the finger the thicker the thumb(it's
whirl,
girls)
round and round

early to better is wiser for worse.
Give
liz
   (take!
tommy)we
order a steak and they send us a pie(it's
try,
boys)
mine is yours

ask me the name of the moon in the man.
Up
sam
   (down!
alice)a
hole in the ocean will never be missed(it's
in,
girls)
yours is mine

either was deafer than neither was dumb.
Skip
fred
   (jump!
neddy)but
under the wonder is over the why(it's
now,
boys)
here we come

2 8

there are possibly 2½ or impossibly 3
individuals every several fat
thousand years. Expecting more would be
neither fantastic nor pathological but

dumb. The number of times a wheel turns
doesn't determine its roundness:if swallows tryst
in your barn be glad;nobody ever earns
anything,everything little looks big in a mist

and if(by Him Whose blood was for us spilled)
than all mankind something more small occurs
or something more distorting than socalled
civilization i'll kiss a stalinist arse

in hitler's window on wednesday next at 1
E.S.T. bring the kiddies let's all have fun

29

anyone lived in a pretty how town
(with up so floating many bells down)
spring summer autumn winter
he sang his didn't he danced his did.

Women and men(both little and small)
cared for anyone not at all
they sowed their isn't they reaped their same
sun moon stars rain

children guessed(but only a few
and down they forgot as up they grew
autumn winter spring summer)
that noone loved him more by more

when by now and tree by leaf
she laughed his joy she cried his grief
bird by snow and stir by still
anyone's any was all to her

someones married their everyones
laughed their cryings and did their dance
(sleep wake hope and then)they
said their nevers they slept their dream

stars rain sun moon
(and only the snow can begin to explain
how children are apt to forget to remember
with up so floating many bells down)

one day anyone died i guess
(and noone stooped to kiss his face)
busy folk buried them side by side
little by little and was by was

all by all and deep by deep
and more by more they dream their sleep
noone and anyone earth by april
wish by spirit and if by yes.

Women and men(both dong and ding)
summer autumn winter spring
reaped their sowing and went their came
sun moon stars rain

3 0

the silently little blue elephant shyly(he was terri
bly
warped by his voyage from every to no)who
still stands still as found some lost thing(like a
curtain on which tiny the was painted in round
blue but quite now it's swirly and foldish so only through)the
little blue elephant at the zoo(jumbled
to queer this what that a here and
there a peers at you)has(elephant the blue)put some just
a now and now little the(on his quiet
head his magical shoulders him doll
self)hay completely thus or that wispily
is to say according to his perfect
satisfaction vanishing from a this world into bigger
much some out of(not visible to us)whom only his dream
ing own soul looks
and
the is all floatful and remembering

3 1

not time's how(anchored in what mountaining roots
of mere eternity)stupendous if
discoverably disappearing floats
at trillionworlded the ecstatic ease

with which vast my complexly wisdoming friend's
—a fingery treesoul onlying from serene
whom queries not suspected selves of space—
life stands gradually upon four minds

(out of some undering joy and overing grief
nothing arrives a so prodigious am
a so immediate is escorts us home
through never's always until absolute un

gulps the first knowledge of death's wandering guess)
while children climb their eyes to touch his dream

3 2

newlys of silence
(both an only

moon the with star

one moving are twilight
they beyond near)

girlest she slender

is cradling in joy her
flower than now

(softlying wisdoms

enter guess)
childmoon smile to

your breathing doll

3 3

one slipslouch twi
tterstamp
coon wid a plon
kykerplung
guit
ar
    (pleez make me glad)dis

dumdam slamslum slopp
idy wurl
sho am
wick
id id
ar
   (now heer we kum dearie)bud

hooz
gwine ter
hate
dad hurt
fool wurl no gal no
boy
   (day simbully loves id)fer

ids dare
pain dares un
no
budy elses un ids
dare dare
joy
   (eye kinely thank yoo)

34

my father moved through dooms of love
through sames of am through haves of give,
singing each morning out of each night
my father moved through depths of height

this motionless forgetful where
turned at his glance to shining here;
that if(so timid air is firm)
under his eyes would stir and squirm

newly as from unburied which
floats the first who,his april touch
drove sleeping selves to swarm their fates
woke dreamers to their ghostly roots

and should some why completely weep
my father's fingers brought her sleep:
vainly no smallest voice might cry
for he could feel the mountains grow.

Lifting the valleys of the sea
my father moved through griefs of joy;
praising a forehead called the moon
singing desire into begin

joy was his song and joy so pure
a heart of star by him could steer
and pure so now and now so yes
the wrists of twilight would rejoice

keen as midsummer's keen beyond
conceiving mind of sun will stand,
so strictly(over utmost him
so hugely)stood my father's dream

his flesh was flesh his blood was blood:
no hungry man but wished him food;
no cripple wouldn't creep one mile
uphill to only see him smile.

Scorning the pomp of must and shall
my father moved through dooms of feel;
his anger was as right as rain
his pity was as green as grain

septembering arms of year extend
less humbly wealth to foe and friend
than he to foolish and to wise
offered immeasurable is

proudly and(by octobering flame
beckoned)as earth will downward climb,
so naked for immortal work
his shoulders marched against the dark

his sorrow was as true as bread:
no liar looked him in the head;
if every friend became his foe
he'd laugh and build a world with snow.

My father moved through theys of we,
singing each new leaf out of each tree
(and every child was sure that spring
danced when she heard my father sing)

then let men kill which cannot share,
let blood and flesh be mud and mire,
scheming imagine,passion willed,
freedom a drug that's bought and sold

giving to steal and cruel kind,
a heart to fear,to doubt a mind,
to differ a disease of same,
conform the pinnacle of am

though dull were all we taste as bright,
bitter all utterly things sweet,
maggoty minus and dumb death
all we inherit,all bequeath

and nothing quite so least as truth
—i say though hate were why men breathe—
because my father lived his soul
love is the whole and more than all

3 5

you which could grin three smiles into a dead
house clutch between eyes emptiness toss one

at nobody shoulder and thick stickingly un

stride after glide massacre monday did
more)ask a lifelump buried by the star
nicked ends next among broken odds of yes
terday's tomorrow(than today can guess

or fears to dare whatever dares to fear)

i very humbly thank you which could grin
may stern particular Love surround your trite
how terrible selfhood with its hands and feet

(lift and may pitying Who from sharp soft worms

of spiralling why and out of black because
your absolute courage with its legs and arms

36

i say no world

can hold a you
shall see the not
because
and why but
(who
stood within his steam beginning and
began to sing all
here is hands machine no

good too quick i know this
suit you pay
a store too
much yes what
too much o much cheap
me i work i know i say i have
not any
never
no vacation here

is hands is work since i am
born is good
but there this cheap this suit too
quick no suit there every
-thing
nothing i
say the
world not fit
you)he is

not(i say the world
yes any world is much
too not quite big enough to
hold one tiny this with
time's
more than
most how
immeasurable
anguish

pregnant one fearless
one good yes
completely kind
mindheart one true one generous child-
man
-god one eager
souldoll one
unsellable not buyable alive
one i say human being)one

goldberger

37

these children singing in stone a
silence of stone these
little children wound with stone
flowers opening for

ever these silently lit
tle children are petals
their song is a flower of
always their flowers

of stone are
silently singing
a song more silent
than silence these always

children forever
singing wreathed with singing
blossoms children of
stone with blossoming

eyes
know if a
lit tle
tree listens

forever to always children singing forever
a song made
of silent as stone silence of
song

3 8

love is the every only god

who spoke this earth so glad and big
even a thing all small and sad
man,may his mighty briefness dig

for love beginning means return
seas who could sing so deep and strong

one queerying wave will whitely yearn
from each last shore and home come young

so truly perfectly the skies
by merciful love whispered were,
completes its brightness with your eyes

any illimitable star

39

denied night's face
have shadowless they?
i bring you peace
the moon of day

predicted end
who never began
of god and fiend?
i give you man

extracted hate
from whispering grass?
joy in time shut
and starved on space?

love's murdered eye
dissected to mere
because and why?
take this whole tear.

By handless hints
do conjurers rule?
do mannikins
forbid the soul?

is death a whore
with life's disease
which quacks will cure
when pimps may please?

must through unstrange
synthetic now
true histories plunge?
rains a grey snow

of mothery same
rotting keen dream?
i rise which am
the sun of whom

40

a peopleshaped toomany-ness far too

and will it tell us who we are and will
it tell us why we dream and will it tell
us how we drink crawl eat walk die fly do?

a notalive undead too-nearishness

and shall we cry and shall we laugh and shall
entirely our doom steer his great small
wish into upward deepness of less fear
much than more climbing hope meets most despair?

all knowing's having and have is(you guess)
perhaps the very unkindest way to kill
each of those creatures called one's self so we'll

not have(but i imagine that yes is
the only living thing)and we'll make yes

41

up into the silence the green
silence with a white earth in it

you will(kiss me)go

out into the morning the young
morning with a warm world in it

(kiss me)you will go

on into the sunlight the fine
sunlight with a firm day in it

you will go(kiss me

down into your memory and
a memory and memory

i)kiss me(will go)

4 2

love is more thicker than forget
more thinner than recall
more seldom than a wave is wet
more frequent than to fail

it is most mad and moonly
and less it shall unbe
than all the sea which only
is deeper than the sea

love is less always than to win
less never than alive
less bigger than the least begin
less littler than forgive

it is most sane and sunly
and more it cannot die
than all the sky which only
is higher than the sky

4 3

hate blows a bubble of despair into
hugeness world system universe and bang
—fear buries a tomorrow under woe
and up comes yesterday most green and young

pleasure and pain are merely surfaces
(one itself showing,itself hiding one)
life's only and true value neither is
love makes the little thickness of the coin

comes here a man would have from madame death
neverless now and without winter spring?
she'll spin that spirit her own fingers with
and give him nothing(if he should not sing)

how much more than enough for both of us
darling. And if i sing you are my voice,

44

air,

be
comes
or

(a)

new
(live)
now

;&

th
(is no littler
th

an a:

fear no bigger
th
an a

hope)is

st
anding
st

a.r

45

enters give
whose lost is his found
leading love
whose heart is her mind)

supremely whole
uplifting the,
of each where all
was is to be

welcomes welcomes
her dreams his face
(her face his dreams
rejoice rejoice)

—opens the sun:
who music wear
burst icy known
swim ignorant fire

(adventuring
and time's dead which;
falling falling
both locked in each

down a thief by
a whore dragged goes
to meet her why
she his because

46

grEEn's d

an
cing on hollow was

young Up
floatingly clothes tumbledish
olD(with

sprouts o
ver and)a-
live
wanders remembe

r
ing per
F
ectl
y

crumb
ling eye
-holes oUt of whe
reful whom(leas

tly)
smiles the
infinite nothing

of
M

an

47

   (sitting in a tree-)
   o small you
   sitting in a tree-

   sitting in a treetop

   riding on a greenest

   riding on a greener
   (o little i)
   riding on a leaf

   o least who
   sing small thing
   dance little joy

   (shine most prayer)

48

mortals)

climbi
       ng i
       nto eachness begi
       n
dizzily
         swingthings
of speeds of
trapeze gush somersaults
open ing
           hes shes
&meet&
        swoop
              fully is are ex
                        quisite theys of re
turn
     a
     n
     d
fall which now drop who all dreamlike

(im

49

       i am so glad and very
       merely my fourth will cure
       the laziest self of weary
       the hugest sea of shore

       so far your nearness reaches
       a lucky fifth of you
       turns people into eachs
       and cowards into grow

our can'ts were born to happen
our mosts have died in more
our twentieth will open
wide a wide open door

we are so both and oneful
night cannot be so sky
sky cannot be so sunful
i am through you so i

5 0

what freedom's not some under's mere above
but breathing yes which fear will never no?
measureless our pure living complete love
whose doom is beauty and its fate to grow

shall hate confound the wise? doubt blind the brave?
does mask wear face? have singings gone to say?
here youngest selves yet younger selves conceive
here's music's music and the day of day

are worlds collapsing? any was a glove
but i'm and you are actual either hand
is when for sale? forever is to give
and on forever's very now we stand

nor a first rose explodes but shall increase
whole truthful infinite immediate us

1 x 1

(One Times One)

1

I

nonsun blob a
cold to
skylessness
sticking fire

my are your
are birds our all
and one gone
away the they

leaf of ghosts some
few creep there
here or on
unearth

I I

neither could say
(it comes so slow
not since not why)
both didn't know

exeunt they
(not false not true
not you not i)
it comes so who

III

it's over a(see just
over this)wall
the apples are(yes
they're gravensteins)all
as red as to lose
and as round as to find.

Each why of a leaf says
(floating each how)
you're which as to die
(each green of a new)
you're who as to grow
but you're he as to do

what must(whispers)be must
be(the wise fool)
if living's to give
so breathing's to steal—
five wishes are five
and one hand is a mind

then over our thief goes
(you go and i)
has pulled(for he's we)
such fruit from what bough
that someone called they
made him pay with his now.

But over a(see just
over this)wall
the red and the round
(they're gravensteins)fall
with kind of a blind
big sound on the ground

IV

of all the blessings which to man
kind progress doth impart
one stands supreme i mean the an
imal without a heart.

Huge this collective pseudobeast
(sans either pain or joy)
does nothing except preexist
its hoi in its polloi

and if sometimes he's prodded forth
to exercise her vote
(or made by threats of something worth
than death to change their coat

—which something as you'll never guess
in fifty thousand years
equals the quote and unquote loss
of liberty my dears—

or even is compelled to fight
itself from tame to teem)
still doth our hero contemplate
in raptures of undream

that strictly(and how)scienti
fic land of supernod
where freedom is compulsory
and only man is god.

Without a heart the animal
is very very kind
so kind it wouldn't like a soul
and couldn't use a mind

V

squints a blond
job at her
diamond
solitaire

while guesswho nibbles his ton of torse

squirms a pool
of pink fat
screams a hole
in it

that birth was wicked and life is worse

squats a big
dove on g
w's wig
so what he

is much too busy sitting the horse

V I

my(his from daughter's mother's zero mind
fahrenheit)old infrequently more and
more much(as aprils elsewhere stroll)exhumed

most innocently undecaying friend
hangs at yon gilty ceiling per both pale
orbs thus excluding a leanderless

drowning in sub(at the next)nakedness
(table but three)hero's carnivorous(smile
by lipstick smell by matchabelli)tits

as(while thumb a plus fingers all with blind
him of who)i discreetly(masturbates
one honest breadcrumb)say "i understand

quite what you mean by"
                                    sold!to the dollarfull shea
with a weakness for living literature
                                    "loyaltea"

VII

ygUDuh

ydoan
yunnuhstan

ydoan o
yunnuhstan dem
yguduh ged

yunnuhstan dem doidee
yguduh ged riduh
ydoan o nudn
LISN bud LISN

dem
gud
am

lidl yelluh bas
tuds weer goin

duhSIVILEYEzum

VIII

applaws)

"fell
ow
sit
isn'ts"

(a paw s

I X

a salesman is an it that stinks Excuse

Me whether it's president of the you were say
or a jennelman name misder finger isn't
important whether it's millions of other punks
or just a handful absolutely doesn't
matter and whether it's in lonjewray

or shrouds is immaterial it stinks

a salesman is an it that stinks to please

but whether to please itself or someone else
makes no more difference than if it sells
hate condoms education snakeoil vac
uumcleaners terror strawberries democ
ra(caveat emptor)cy superfluous hair

or Think We've Met subhuman rights Before

X

a politician is an arse upon
which everyone has sat except a man

X I

mr u will not be missed
who as an anthologist
sold the many on the few
not excluding mr u

XII

it was a goodly co
which paid to make man free
(for man is enslaved by a dread dizziz
and the sooner it's over the sooner to biz
don't ask me what it's pliz)

then up rose bishop budge from kew
a anglican was who
(with a rag and a bone and a hank of hair)'d
he picked up a thousand pounds or two
and he smote the monster merde

then up rose pride and up rose pelf
and ghibelline and guelph
and ladios and laddios
(on radios and raddios)
did save man from himself

ye duskiest despot's goldenest gal
did wring that dragon's tail
(for men must loaf and women must lay)
and she gave him a desdemonial
that took his breath away

all history oped her teeming womb
said demon for to doom
yea(fresh complexions being oke
with him)one william shakespeare broke
the silence of the tomb

then up rose mr lipshits pres
(who always nothing says)
and he kisséd the general menedjerr
and they smokéd a robert burns cigerr
to the god of things like they err

XIII

plato told

him:he couldn't
believe it(jesus

told him;he
wouldn't believe
it)lao

tsze
certainly told
him,and general
(yes

mam)
sherman;
and even
(believe it
or

not)you
told him:i told
him;we told him
(he didn't believe it,no

sir)it took
a nipponized bit of
the old sixth

avenue
el;in the top of his head:to tell

him

XIV

pity this busy monster,manunkind,

not. Progress is a comfortable disease:
your victim(death and life safely beyond)

plays with the bigness of his littleness
—electrons deify one razorblade
into a mountainrange;lenses extend

unwish through curving wherewhen till unwish
returns on its unself.
               A world of made
is not a world of born—pity poor flesh

and trees,poor stars and stones,but never this
fine specimen of hypermagical

ultraomnipotence. We doctors know

a hopeless case if—listen:there's a hell
of a good universe next door;let's go

XV

("fire stop thief help murder save the world"

what world?
            is it themselves these insects mean?
when microscopic shriekings shall have snarled
threads of celestial silence huger than
eternity,men will be saviours
                    —flop
grasshopper,exactly nothing's soon;
scream,all ye screamers,till your if is up
and vanish under prodigies of un)

"have you" the mountain,while his maples wept
air to blood,asked "something a little child
who's just as small as me can do or be?"
god whispered him a snowflake "yes:you may
sleep now,my mountain" and this mountain slept

while his pines lifted their green lives and smiled

X V I

one's not half two. It's two are halves of one:
which halves reintegrating,shall occur
no death and any quantity;but than
all numerable mosts the actual more

minds ignorant of stern miraculous
this every truth—beware of heartless them
(given the scalpel,they dissect a kiss;
or,sold the reason,they undream a dream)

one is the song which fiends and angels sing:
all murdering lies by mortals told make two.
Let liars wilt,repaying life they're loaned;
we(by a gift called dying born)must grow

deep in dark least ourselves remembering
love only rides his year.
                          All lose,whole find

XVII

one(Floatingly)arrive

(silent)one by(alive)
from(into disappear

and perfectly)nowhere
vivid anonymous
mythical guests of Is

unslowly more who(and
here who there who)descend
-ing(mercifully)touch
deathful earth's any which

Weavingly now one by
wonder(on twilight)they
come until(over dull

all nouns)begins a whole
verbal adventure to

illimitably Grow

XVIII

as any(men's hells having wrestled with)
man drops into his own paradise
thankfully
            whole and the green whereless truth
of an eternal now welcomes each was
of whom among not numerable ams

(leaving a perfectly distinct unhe;
a ticking phantom by prodigious time's
mere brain contrived:a spook of stop and go)
may i achieve another steepest thing—

how more than sleep illimitably my
—being so very born no bird can sing
as easily creation up all sky

(really unreal world,will you perhaps do
the breathing for me while i am away?)

XIX

when you are silent,shining host by guest
a snowingly enfolding glory is

all angry common things to disappear
causing through mystery miracle peace:

or(if begin the colours of your voice)
from some complete existence of to dream
into complete some dream of to exist
a stranger who is i awakening am.

Living no single thing dares partly seem
one atomy once,and every cannot stir
imagining;while you are motionless—

whose moving is more april than the year
(if all her most first little flowers rise

out of tremendous darkness into air)

XX

what if a much of a which of a wind
gives the truth to summer's lie;
bloodies with dizzying leaves the sun
and yanks immortal stars awry?
Blow king to beggar and queen to seem
(blow friend to fiend:blow space to time)
—when skies are hanged and oceans drowned,
the single secret will still be man

what if a keen of a lean wind flays
screaming hills with sleet and snow:
strangles valleys by ropes of thing
and stifles forests in white ago?
Blow hope to terror;blow seeing to blind
(blow pity to envy and soul to mind)
—whose hearts are mountains,roots are trees,
it's they shall cry hello to the spring

what if a dawn of a doom of a dream
bites this universe in two,
peels forever out of his grave
and sprinkles nowhere with me and you?
Blow soon to never and never to twice
(blow life to isn't:blow death to was)
—all nothing's only our hugest home;
the most who die,the more we live

XXI

dead every enormous piece
of nonsense which itself must call
a state submicroscopic is—
compared with pitying terrible
some alive individual

ten centuries of original soon
or make it ten times ten are more
than not entitled to complain
—plunged in eternal now if who're
by the five nevers of a lear

XXII

no man,if men are gods;but if gods must
be men,the sometimes only man is this
(most common,for each anguish is his grief;
and,for his joy is more than joy,most rare)

a fiend,if fiends speak truth;if angels burn

by their own generous completely light,
an angel;or(as various worlds he'll spurn
rather than fail immeasurable fate)
coward,clown,traitor,idiot,dreamer,beast—

such was a poet and shall be and is

—who'll solve the depths of horror to defend
a sunbeam's architecture with his life:
and carve immortal jungles of despair
to hold a mountain's heartbeat in his hand

XXIII

love is a spring at which
crazy they drink who've climbed
steeper than hopes are fears
only not ever named
mountains more if than each
known allness disappears

lovers are mindless they
higher than fears are hopes
lovers are those who kneel
lovers are these whose lips
smash unimagined sky
deeper than heaven is hell

XXIV

(once like a spark)

if strangers meet
life begins—
not poor not rich
(only aware)
kind neither
nor cruel
(only complete)
i not not you
not possible;
only truthful
—truthfully,once
if strangers(who
deep our most are
selves)touch:
forever

(and so to dark)

XXV

what over and which under
burst lurch things phantoms curl
(mouth seekingly lips wander
a finding whom of girl)

dolls clutching their dolls wallow
toys playing writhe with toys
(than are all unworlds hollow
silence has deeper eyes

purest than fear's obscener
brightest than hate's more black
keenest than dying's keener
each will kissed breast awake)

slow tottering visions bigly
come crashing into go
(all than were nevers ugly
beautiful most is now)

XXVI

when god decided to invent
everything he took one
breath bigger than a circustent
and everything began

when man determined to destroy
himself he picked the was
of shall and finding only why
smashed it into because

XXVII

old mr ly
fresh from a fu
ruddy as a sun
with blue true two

man
neral
rise
eyes

"this world's made 'bout
right it's the people that
abuses it you can git
anything you like out

of it if
you gut a mind
to there's something
for everybody it's a"

old mr lyman
ruddy as a sunrise
fresh with blue come
true from

a funeral
eyes
"big
thing"

XXVIII

rain or hail
sam done
the best he kin
till they digged his hole

:sam was a man

stout as a bridge
rugged as a bear
slickern a weazel
how be you

(sun or snow)

gone into what
like all them kings
you read about
and on him sings

a whippoorwill;

heart was big
as the world aint square
with room for the devil
and his angels too

yes,sir

what may be better
or what may be worse
and what may be clover
clover clover

(nobody'll know)

sam was a man
grinned his grin
done his chores
laid him down.

Sleep well

XXIX

let it go—the
smashed word broken
open vow or
the oath cracked length
wise—let it go it
was sworn to

       go

let them go—the
truthful liars and
the false fair friends
and the boths and
neithers—you must let them go they
were born

       to go

let all go—the
big small middling
tall bigger really
the biggest and all
things—let all go
dear

       so comes love

XXX

Hello is what a mirror says
it is a maid says Who
and(hearing not a which)replies
in haste I must be you

no sunbeam ever lies

Bang is the meaning of a gun
it is a man means No
and(seeing something yes)will grin
with pain You so&so

true wars are never won

XXXI

a-

float on some
?
i call twilight you

'll see

an in
-ch
of an if

&

who
is
the

)

more
dream than become
more

am than imagine

XXXII

i've come to ask you if there isn't a
new moon outside your window saying if

that's all,just if"
                    "that's all there is to say"

(and she looked)"especially in winter"(like a leaf
opening)
            as we stood,one(truthed
by wisping tinily the silverest

alive silentness god ever breathed

upon beginning)
           "beautiful o most
beautiful" her,my life worships and
(night)
      then "everything beautiful can grow"

my,her life marvels "here'll be a canoe

and a whole world and then a single hair
again" marvels "and liars kill their kind

but" her,my "love creates love only" our

XXXIII

    open green those
    (dear)
    worlds of than great
    more eyes,and what
    were summer's beside their
    glories

    downward if they'll
    or
    goldenly float
    so(dreaming out
    of dreams among)no year
    will fall

    this than,a least
    dare
    of snow less quite
    is nothing but
    herself,and than this(mere
    most)breast

    spring's million(who
    are
    and do not wait)
    buds imitate
    upward each first flower
    of two

XXXIV

nothing false and possible is love
(who's imagined,therefore limitless)
love's to giving as to keeping's give;
as yes is to if,love is to yes

must's a schoolroom in the month of may:
life's the deathboard where all now turns when
(love's a universe beyond obey
or command,reality or un-)

proudly depths above why's first because
(faith's last doubt and humbly heights below)
kneeling,we—true lovers—pray that us
will ourselves continue to outgrow

all whose mosts if you have known and i've
only we our least begin to guess

XXXV

except in your
honour,
my loveliest,
nothing
may move may rest
—you bring

(out of dark the
earth)a
procession of
wonders
huger than prove
our fears

were hopes:the moon
open
for you and close
will shy
wings of because;
each why

of star(afloat
on not
quite less than all
of time)
gives you skilful
his flame

so is your heart
alert,
of languages
there's none
but well she knows;
and can

perfectly speak
(snowflake
and rainbow mind
and soul
november and
april)

who younger than
begin
are,the worlds move
in your
(and rest,my love)
honour

XXXVI

true lovers in each happening of their hearts
live longer than all which and every who;
despite what fear denies,what hope asserts,
what falsest both disprove by proving true

(all doubts,all certainties,as villains strive
and heroes through the mere mind's poor pretend
—grim comics of duration:only love
immortally occurs beyond the mind)

such a forever is love's any now
and her each here is such an everywhere,
even more true would truest lovers grow
if out of midnight dropped more suns than are

(yes;and if time should ask into his was
all shall,their eyes would never miss a yes)

XXXVII

we love each other very dearly
                              ,more
than raindrops need sunbeams or snowflakes make
possible mayflowers:

                         quite eyes of air
not with twilight's first thrushes may awake
more secretly than our(if disappear
should some world)selves

                      .No doing shall undo
(nor madness nor mere death nor both who is
la guerre)your me or simplify my you
                              ,darling

            sweet this creative never known
complexity was born before the moon
before God wished Himself into a rose

and even(
            we'll adventure the into
most immemorial of whens
)before

each heartbeat which i am alive to kiss

XXXVIII

yes is a pleasant country:
if's wintry
(my lovely)
let's open the year

both is the very weather
(not either)
my treasure,
when violets appear

love is a deeper season
than reason;
my sweet one
(and april's where we're)

XXXIX

all ignorance toboggans into know
and trudges up to ignorance again:
but winter's not forever,even snow
melts;and if spring should spoil the game,what then?

all history's a winter sport or three:
but were it five,i'd still insist that all
history is too small for even me;
for me and you,exceedingly too small.

Swoop(shrill collective myth)into thy grave
merely to toil the scale to shrillerness
per every madge and mabel dick and dave
—tomorrow is our permanent address

and there they'll scarcely find us(if they do,
we'll move away still further:into now

X L

darling!because my blood can sing
and dance(and does with each your least
your any most very amazing now
or here)let pitiless fear play host
to every isn't that's under the spring
—but if a look should april me,
down isn't's own isn't go ghostly they

doubting can turn men's see to stare
their faith to how their joy to why
their stride and breathing to limp and prove
—but if a look should april me,
some thousand million hundred more
bright worlds than merely by doubting have
darkly themselves unmade makes love

armies(than hate itself and no
meanness unsmaller)armies can
immensely meet for centuries
and(except nothing)nothing's won
—but if a look should april me
for half a when,whatever is less
alive than never begins to yes

but if a look should april me
(though such as perfect hope can feel
only despair completely strikes
forests of mind,mountains of soul)
quite at the hugest which of his who
death is killed dead. Hills jump with brooks:
trees tumble out of twigs and sticks;

1

XLI

how

tinily
of

squir(two be
tween sto
nes)ming a gr

eenes
t you b
ecome

s whi
(mysterious
ly)te

one
t

hou

XLII

might these be thrushes climbing through almost(do they

beautifully wandering in merciful
miracles wonderingly celebrate day
and welcome earth's arrival with a soul)

sunlight?yes
                    (always we have heard them sing
the dark alive but)
                    look:begins to grow
more than all real,all imagining;

and we who are we?surely not i not you
behold nor any breathing creature this?
nothing except the impossible shall occur

—see!now himself uplifts of stars the star
(sing!every joy)—wholly now disappear
night's not eternal terrors like a guess.

Life's life and strikes my your our blossoming sphere

XLIII

if(among
silent skies
bluer than believing)a
little gay
earth opening
is all the flowers of his eyes
:april's they

this if now
or this(young
trembling any)into flame
twig or limb
explodes and o
each living ablaze greenly thing
;may has come

love(by yes
every new
bird no bigger than to sing)
leaf is wing
and tree is voice
more leastfully than i am you
,we are spring

XLIV

these(whom;pretends

blue nothing)
are
built of soon carved
of to born of
be

One

:petals
him starrily her
and around
ing swim
snowing

ly upward with **Joy,**

no
where(no)when
may
breathe
so sky so

.wish

XLV

i think you like"

a strawberry
bang this
blueeyed world(on
which are wintry

handlebars

glued)updives pursued
by its wigglesome whisperful
body and
almost

isn't(grabbed into skies of

grin)"my
flowers"(the humble
man than sunlight
older with ships than

dreams more hands are

offering jonquils)down again
who but zooms
through
one perfectly beautiful bow

"my home ionian isles

X L V I

open your heart:
i'll give you a treasure
of tiniest world
a piece of forever with

summitless younger than
angels are mountains
rivery forests
towerful towns(queen

poet king float
sprout heroes of moonstar
flutter to and
swim blossoms of person)through

musical shadows while hunted
by daemons
seethe luminous
leopards(on wingfeet of thingfear)

come ships go
snowily sailing
perfect silence.
Absolute ocean

XLVII

until and i heard
a certain a bird
i dreamed i could sing
but like nothing
                    are the joys
of his voice

until and who came
with a song like a dream
of a bird with a song
like not anything
                    under skies
over grass

until and until
into flame i can feel
how the earth must fly
if a truth is a cry
                    of a whole
of a soul

until i awoke
for the beautiful sake
of a grave gay brave
bright cry of alive
                    with a trill
        like until

XLVIII

so isn't small one littlest why,
it into if shall climb all the
blue heaven green earth neither sea
here's more than room for three of me

and only while your sweet eyes close
have disappeared a million whys;
but opening if are those eyes
every because is murdered twice

XLIX

trees
      were in(give
give)bud when to me
you
made for by love
love said did
o no yes

earth was in
              (live
live)spring
with all beautiful
things when to
me
you gave gave darling

birds are
         in(trees are in)
song
when to me you
leap and i'm born we
're sunlight of
oneness

L

which is the very
(in sad this havingest
world)most merry
most fair most rare
—the livingest givingest
girl on this whirlingest
earth?
                why you're
by far the darlingest

who(on this busily
nowhere rollingest
it)'s the dizzily
he most him
—the climbingly fallingest
fool in this trickiest
if?
        why i'm
by much the luckiest

what of the wonder
(beingest growingest)
over all under
all hate all fear
—all perfectly dyingest
my and foreverless
thy?
        why our
is love and neverless

L I

"sweet spring is your
time is my time is our
time for springtime is lovetime
and viva sweet love"

(all the merry little birds are
flying in the floating in the
very spirits singing in
are winging in the blossoming)

lovers go and lovers come
awandering awondering
but any two are perfectly
alone there's nobody else alive

(such a sky and such a sun
i never knew and neither did you
and everybody never breathed
quite so many kinds of yes)

not a tree can count his leaves
each herself by opening
but shining who by thousands mean
only one amazing thing

(secretly adoring shyly
tiny winging darting floating
merry in the blossoming
always joyful selves are singing)

"sweet spring is your
time is my time is our
time for springtime is lovetime
and viva sweet love"

LII

life is more true than reason will deceive
(more secret or than madness did reveal)
deeper is life than lose:higher than have
—but beauty is more each than living's all

multiplied with infinity sans if
the mightiest meditations of mankind
cancelled are by one merely opening leaf
(beyond whose nearness there is no beyond)

or does some littler bird than eyes can learn
look up to silence and completely sing?
futures are obsolete;pasts are unborn
(here less than nothing's more than everything)

death,as men call him,ends what they call men
—but beauty is more now than dying's when

LIII

o by the by
has anybody seen
little you-i
who stood on a green
hill and threw
his wish at blue

with a swoop and a dart
out flew his wish
(it dived like a fish
but it climbed like a dream)
throbbing like a heart
singing like a flame

blue took it my
far beyond far
and high beyond high
bluer took it your
but bluest took it our
away beyond where

what a wonderful thing
is the end of a string
(murmurs little you-i
as the hill becomes nil)
and will somebody tell
me why people let go

LIV

if everything happens that can't be done
(and anything's righter
than books
could plan)
the stupidest teacher will almost guess
(with a run
skip
around we go yes)
there's nothing as something as one

one hasn't a why or because or although
(and buds know better
than books
don't grow)
one's anything old being everything new
(with a what
which
around we come who)
one's everyanything so

so world is a leaf so tree is a bough
(and birds sing sweeter
than books
tell how)
so here is away and so your is a my
(with a down
up
around again fly)
forever was never till now

now i love you and you love me
(and books are shuter
than books
can be)
and deep in the high that does nothing but fall
(with a shout
each
around we go all)
there's somebody calling who's we

we're anything brighter than even the sun
(we're everything greater
than books
might mean)
we're everyanything more than believe
(with a spin
leap
alive we're alive)
we're wonderful one times one

marion's book

XAIPE

to
hildegarde
watson

1

this(let's remember)day died again and
again;whose golden,crimson dooms conceive

an oceaning abyss of orange dream

larger than sky times earth:a flame beyond
soul immemorially forevering am—
and as collapsing that grey mind by wave
doom disappeared,out of perhaps(who knows?)

eternity floated a blossoming

(while anyone might slowly count to soon)
rose—did you see her?darling,did you(kiss
me)quickly count to never?you were wrong

—then all the way from perfect nowhere came

(as easily as we forget something)
livingest the imaginable moon

2

hush)
noones
are coming
out in the gloam
ing together are
standing together un
der a particular tree
are all breathing bright darkness to
gether are slowly all together

very magically smiling and if

we are not perfectly careful be
lieve me you and i'll go strolling
right through these each illimit
able to speak very
softly altogeth
er miracu
lous citi
zens of
(hush

3

purer than purest pure
whisper of a whisper

so(big with innocence)
forgivingly a once
of eager glory,no
more miracle may grow

—childfully serious
flower of holiness

a pilgrim from beyond
the future's future;and
immediate like some
newly remembered dream—

flaming a coolly bell
touches most mere until

(eternally)with(now)
luminous the shadow
of love himself:who's we
—nor can you die or i

and every world,before
silence begins a star

4

this out of within itself moo
ving lump of twilight squirts a two
ne like nothing verdi slightly knu

as and some six cents hit the whigh
shaped hathole thangew yelps one shi
ly glad old unman who is eye

5

swim so now million many worlds in each

least less than particle of perfect dark—
how should a loudness called mankind unteach
whole infinite the who of life's life(hark!

what silence)?" "Worlds?o no:i'm certain they're
(look again)flowers." "Don't worlds open and
worlds close?" "Worlds do, but differently;or

as if worlds wanted us to understand
they'd never close(and open)if that fool
called everyone(or you or i)were wise."

"You mean worlds may have better luck,some day?"
"Or worse!poor worlds;i mean they're possible
—but" lifting "flowers" more all stars than eyes

"only are quite what worlds merely might be

6

dying is fine)but Death

?o
baby
i

wouldn't like

Death if Death
were
good:for

when(instead of stopping to think)you

begin to feel of it,dying
's miraculous
why?be

cause dying is

perfectly natural;perfectly
putting
it mildly lively(but

Death

is strictly
scientific
& artificial &

evil & legal)

we thank thee
god
almighty for dying

(forgive us,o life!the sin of Death

7

we miss you,jack—tactfully you(with one cocked
eyebrow)subtracting clichés un by un
till the god's truth stands art-naked:you and the fact

that rotgut never was brewed which could knock you down

(while scotch was your breakfast every night all day)
a 3ringbrain you had and a circusheart
and we miss them more than any bright word may cry
—even the crackling spark of(hung in a)"fert

ig"
    (tent-sky wholly wallendas)
                         ready were all

erect your yous to cross the chasm of time
lessness;but two dim disks of stare are still
wondering if the stunt was really a dream—

here's,wherever you aren't or are,good luck!
aberdeen plato-rabelais peter jack

               8

     o

     the round
     little man we
     loved so isn't

     no!w

     a gay of a
     brave and
     a true of a

     who have

     r
     olle
     d i

     nt

     o
     n
     o

     w(he)re

9

possibly thrice we glimpsed—
                           more likely twice
that(once crammed into someone's kitchenette)

wheezing bulgily world of genial plac
-idity(plus,out of much its misbutt-
oned trouserfly tumbling,faded five
or so lightyears of pyjamastring)

a(vastly and particularly)live
that undeluded notselfpitying

lover of all things excellently rare;
obsolete almost that phenomenon
(too gay for malice and too wise for fear)
of shadowy virtue and of sunful sin

namely(ford madox ford)and eke to wit
a human being
                —let's remember that

1 0

or who and who)

The distance is
more much than all
of timely space
(was and be will)
from beautiful

obvious to

Mere but one small
most of a rose
easily(while
will be goes was)
can travel this

or i and you

1 1

so many selves(so many fiends and gods
each greedier than every)is a man
(so easily one in another hides;
yet man can,being all,escape from none)

so huge a tumult is the simplest wish:
so pitiless a massacre the hope
most innocent(so deep's the mind of flesh
and so awake what waking calls asleep)

so never is most lonely man alone
(his briefest breathing lives some planet's year,
his longest life's a heartbeat of some sun;
his least unmotion roams the youngest star)

—how should a fool that calls him "I" presume
to comprehend not numerable whom?

1 2

tw

o o
ld
o

nce upo

n
a(
n

o mo

re
)time
me

n

sit(l
oo
k)dre

am

13

chas sing does(who
,ins
tead,
smiles alw

ays a trifl
e
w
hile ironin

g!
nob odyknowswhos esh
?i
rt)n't

14

out of more find than seeks

thinking,swim(opening)grow
are(me wander and nows to the

power of blueness)whos(ex-
plore my unreal in

-credible true each new

self)smile. Eyes. & we
remember:yes;we played with a piece of when

till it rolled behind forever,we touched a shy
animal called where and she disappeared.

Out of more(fingeryhands

me and whying)seek than finds
feeling(seize)floats(only by

only)a silence only made of,bird

15

hair your a brook
(it through are gaze
the unguessed whys
by me at look)

swirls to engulf
(in which in soft)
firm who outlift
queries of self

pouring(alive
twice)and becomes
eithering dreams
the secret of

16

if the

green
opens
a little a
little
was
much and much
is

too if

the green robe
o
p
e
n
s
and two are

wildstrawberries

1 7

(swooning)a pillar of youngly

loveflesh topped
with danc
ing egghead strutstrolls

eager a(twice

by
Dizzying eyeplums
pun

ctured)moo

nface swimming
ly
dreamseems

(vivi

d
an O
of

milky tranceworld writhes

in
twi
nn

ingly scarlet woundsmile)

1 8

a(ncient)a

weigh
tless

puppet of once
man(clutched
by immense

the-seat-of-the
pants
inani
nvisible Fist)drifts

a
long conway
's

unstreet with
treadwatering

nonlegs(strictly)smiling

1 9

out of the mountain of his soul comes
a keen pure silence)such hands can
build a(who are like ocean patient)dream's

eternity(you feel behind this man
earth's first sunrise)and his voice
is green like growing(is miraculous like
tomorrow)all around the self of this

being are growing stones(neither awake
are goddesses nor sleeping)since he's young
with mysteries(each truly his more than
some eighty years through which that memory strolls)
and every ours for the mere worshipping

(as calmly as if aristide maillols
occurred with any ticking of a clock

2 0

goo-dmore-ning(en

ter)nize-aday(most
gently herculanean

my mortal)yoo

make sno eye kil
yoo(friend the laughing
grinning)we

no(smiling)strike

agains
De Big Boss
(crying)jew wop
rich poor(sing

ing)

He
    no
        care
           so
               what

yoo-gointa-doo?(ice

coal wood
man)nic
he like
wint-air

nic like ot-am

sum-air(young
old nic)
like spring yoo

un-air-stan?me

crazy
me like

evry-ting

2 1

jake hates
            all the girls(the
shy ones,the bold
ones;the meek
proud sloppy sleek)
all except the cold
                        ones

paul scorns all
                    the girls(the
bright ones,the dim
ones;the slim
plump tiny tall)
all except the
                    dull ones

gus loves all the
                        girls(the
warped ones,the lamed
ones;the mad
moronic maimed)
all except
            the dead ones

mike likes all the girls
                            (the
fat ones,the lean
ones;the mean
kind dirty clean)
all
        except the green ones

2 2

when serpents bargain for the right to squirm
and the sun strikes to gain a living wage—
when thorns regard their roses with alarm
and rainbows are insured against old age

when every thrush may sing no new moon in
if all screech-owls have not okayed his voice
—and any wave signs on the dotted line
or else an ocean is compelled to close

when the oak begs permission of the birch
to make an acorn—valleys accuse their
mountains of having altitude—and march
denounces april as a saboteur

then we'll believe in that incredible
unanimal mankind(and not until)

2 3

three wealthy sisters swore they'd never part:
Soul was(i understand)
seduced by Life;whose brother married Heart,
now Mrs Death. Poor Mind

2 4

one day a nigger
caught in his hand
a little star no bigger
than not to understand

"i'll never let you go
until you've made me white"
so she did and now
stars shine at night

2 5

pieces(in darker
than small is dirtiest
any city's least
street)of mirror

lying are each(why
do people say it's un
lucky to break one)
whole with sky

2 6

who sharpens every dull
here comes the only man
reminding with his bell
to disappear a sun

and out of houses pour
maids mothers widows wives
bringing this visitor
their very oldest lives

one pays him with a smile
another with a tear
some cannot pay at all
he never seems to care

he sharpens is to am
he sharpens say to sing
you'd almost cut your thumb
so right he sharpens wrong

and when their lives are keen
he throws the world a kiss
and slings his wheel upon
his back and off he goes

but we can hear him still
if now our sun is gone
reminding with his bell
to reappear a moon

2 7

"summer is over
—it's no use demanding
that lending be giving;
it's no good pretending
befriending means loving"
(sighs mind:and he's clever)
"for all,yes for all
sweet things are until"

"spring follows winter:
as clover knows,maybe"
(heart makes the suggestion)
"or even a daisy—
your thorniest question
my roses will answer"
"but dying's meanwhile"
(mind murmurs;the fool)

"truth would prove truthless
and life a mere pastime
—each joy a deceiver,
and sorrow a system—
if now than forever
could never(by breathless
one breathing)be" soul
"more" cries:with a smile

2 8

noone" autumnal this great lady's gaze

enters a sunset "can grow(gracefully or
otherwise)old. Old may mean anything
which everyone would rather not become;
but growing is" erect her whole life smiled

"was and will always remain:who i am.

Look at these(each serenely welcoming
his only and illimitably his
destiny)mountains!how can each" while flame
crashed "be so am and i and who?each grows"

then in a whisper,as time turned to dream

"and poets grow;and(there—see?)children" nor
might any earth's first morning have concealed
so unimaginably young a star

29

nine birds(rising

through a gold moment)climb:
ing i

-nto
wintry
twi-

light
(all together a
manying
one

-ness)nine
souls
only alive with a single mys-

tery(liftingly
caught upon falling)silent!

ly living the dying of glory

30

snow means that

life is a black cannonadin
g into silenc
e go

lliw

og-dog)life
?
tree3ghosts

are Is A eyes

Strange
known
Face

(whylaughing!among:skydiamonds

3 1

infinite jukethrob smoke & swallow to dis

gorge)
        a sulky gob with entirely white
eyes of elsewhere
                        jabber while(infinite
fog & puking jukepulse hug)large less
than more magnetic pink unwhores
                                a wai
ter lugs his copious whichwhat skilfully here
&(simply infinite)there &
                        (smoke)a fair
y socked flopslump(& juke)ing shrieks Yew May
n't Dew Thiz Tew Mee
                        as somebody's almost moth
er folds(but infinite)gently up
                        the with
a carroty youth blonde whis(gorgedis reswal
lowing spewnonspew clutch)pers again & again
(jukejog mist & strict)
                & again
                        (ly infin)

It's Snowing Isn't That Perfectly Wonderful

3 2

blossoming are people

nimbler than Really
go whirling into gaily

white thousands return

by millions and dreaming

drift hundreds come swimming
(Each a keener secret

than silence even tells)

all the earth has turned to sky

are flowers neither why nor how
when is now and which is Who

and i am you are i am we

(pretty twinkle merry bells)

Someone has been born
everyone is noone

dance around the snowman

3 3

if a cheerfulest Elephantangelchild should sit

(holding a red candle over his head
by a finger of trunk,and singing out of a red

book)on a proud round cloud in a white high night

where his heartlike ears have flown adorable him
self tail and all(and his tail's red christmas bow)
—and if,when we meet again,little he(having flown
even higher)is sunning his penguinsoul in the glow

of a joy which wasn't and isn't and won't be words

while possibly not(at a guess)quite half way down
to the earth are leapandswooping tinily birds
whose magical gaiety makes your beautiful name—

i feel that(false and true are merely to know)
Love only has ever been,is,and will ever be,So

34

a thrown a

-way It
with some-
thing sil
-very

;bright,&:mys(

a thrown a-
way
X
-mas)ter-

i

-ous wisp A of glo-
ry.pr
-ettily
cl(tr)in(ee)gi-

ng

35

light's lives lurch
        a once world quickly from rises

army the gradual of unbeing(fro
on stiffening greenly air and to ghosts go
drift slippery hands tease slim float twitter faces)
only stand with me,love!against these its
until you are and until i am dreams

until comes vast dark until sink last things

(least all turns almost now;now almost swims
into a hair's width:into less?into

not)
      love,stand with me while silence sings

not into nothing and nothing into never
and never into(touch me!love)forever
—until is and shall be and was are night's

total exploding millionminded Who

3 6

quick i the death of thing
glimpsed(and on every side
swoop mountains flimsying
become if who'd)

me under a opens
(of petals of silence)
hole bigger than
never to have been

what above did was
always fall
(yes but behind yes)
without or until

no atom couldn't die
(how and am quick i
they'll all not conceive
less who than love)

3 7

F is for foetus(a

punkslapping
mobsucking
gravypissing poppa but
who just couldn't help it no

matter how hard he never tried)the

great pink
superme
diocri
ty of

a hyperhypocritical D

mocra
c(sing
down with the fascist beast
boom

boom)two eyes

for an eye four
teeth for a tooth
(and the wholly babble open at
blessed are the peacemuckers)

$ $ $ etc(as

the boodle's bent is the
crowd inclined it's
freedom from freedom
the common man wants)

honey swoRkey mollypants

                        3 8
why must itself up every of a park

anus stick some quote statue unquote to
prove that a hero equals any jerk
who was afraid to dare to answer "no"?

quote citizens unquote might otherwise
forget(to err is human;to forgive
divine)that if the quote state unquote says
"kill" killing is an act of christian love.

"Nothing" in 1944 A D

"can stand against the argument of mil
itary necessity"(generalissimo e)
and echo answers "there is no appeal

from reason"(freud)—you pays your money and
you doesn't take your choice. Ain't freedom grand

39

            open his head,baby
            & you'll find a heart in it
            (cracked)

            open that heart,mabel
            & you'll find a bed in it
            (fact)

            open this bed,sibyl
            & you'll find a tart in it
            (wed)

            open the tart,lady
            & you'll find his mind in it
            (dead)

40

        i'm
        asking
        you dear to
        what else could a
        no but it doesn't
        of course but you don't seem
        to realize i can't make
        it clearer war just isn't what
        we imagine but please for god's O
        what the hell yes it's true that was
        me but that me isn't me
        can't you see now no not
        any christ but you
        must understand
        why because
        i am
        dead

41

    whose are these(wraith a clinging with a wraith)

    ghosts drowning in supreme thunder?ours
    (over you reels and me a moon;beneath,

bombed the by ocean earth bigly shudders)

never was death so alive:chaos so(hark
—that screech of space)absolute(my soul
tastes If as some world of a spark

's gulped by illimitable hell)

and never have breathed such miracle murdered we
whom cannot kill more mostful to arrive
each(futuring snowily which sprints for the
crumb of our Now)twiceuponatime wave—

put out your eyes,and touch the black skin
of an angel named imagination

42

neither awake
(there's your general
yas buy gad)
nor asleep

booted & spurred
with an apish grin
(extremely like
but quite absurd

gloved fist on hip
& the scowl of a cannibal)
there's your mineral
general animal

(five foot five)
neither dead
nor alive
(in real the rain)

43

o to be in finland
now that russia's here)

swing low
sweet ca

rr
y on

(pass the freedoms pappy or
uncle shylock not interested

44

where's Jack Was
General Was
the hero of the Battle of Because
    he's squatting
in the middle of remember
with his rotten old forgotten
full of why
    (rub-her-bub)
    bub?
    (bubs)

where's Jim Soon
Admiral Soon
the saviour of the Navy of the Moon
    he's swooning
at the bottom of the ocean
of forever with a never
in his fly
    (rub-her-bub)
    bub?
    (bubs)

where's John Big
Doughgob Big
pastmaster of the Art of Jigajig
    sitting pretty
on the top of notwithstanding
with his censored up a wench's
rock-a-bye
    (rub-her-bub)
    bub?
    (bubs)

45

when your honest redskin toma
hawked and scalped his victim ,

not to save a world for stalin
was he aiming ;

spare the child and spoil the rod
quoth the palmist .

46

a kike is the most dangerous
machine as yet invented
by even yankee ingenu
ity(out of a jew a few
dead dollars and some twisted laws)
it comes both prigged and canted

47

meet mr universe(who clean

and jerked 300 lbs)i mean
observe his these regard his that(sh)

who made the world's best one hand snatch

48

&(all during the

dropsin
king god my sic
kly a thingish o crashdis
appearing con ter fusion ror collap
sing thatthis is whichwhat yell itfulls o
f cringewiltdroolery i
mean really th
underscream of sudde
nly perishing eagerly everyw
here shutting forever&forever fol
ding int
o absolute gone &
positive quite n
ever & bi
g screeching new black perfectly isn

't)one rose opened

49

this is a rubbish of human rind
with a photograph
clutched in the half
of a hand and the word
love underlined

this is a girl who died in her mind
with a warm thick scream
and a keen cold groan
while the gadgets purred
and the gangsters dined

this is a deaf dumb church and blind
with an if in its soul
and a hole in its life
where the young bell tolled
and the old vine twined

this is a dog of no known kind
with one white eye
and one black eye
and the eyes of his eyes
are as lost as you'll find

50

no time ago
or else a life
walking in the dark
i met christ

jesus)my heart
flopped over
and lay still
while he passed(as

close as i'm to you
yes closer
made of nothing
except loneliness

5 1

who were so dark of heart they might not speak,
a little innocence will make them sing;
teach them to see who could not learn to look
—from the reality of all nothing

will actually lift a luminous whole;
turn sheer despairing to most perfect gay,
nowhere to here,never to beautiful:
a little innocence creates a day.

And something thought or done or wished without
a little innocence,although it were
as red as terror and as green as fate,
greyly shall fail and dully disappear—

but the proud power of himself death immense
is not so as a little innocence

5 2

to start,to hesitate;to stop
(kneeling in doubt:while all
skies fall)and then to slowly trust
T upon H,and smile

could anything be pleasanter
(some big dark little day
which seems a lifetime at the least)
except to add an A?

henceforth he feels his pride involved
(this i who's also you)
and nothing less than excellent
E will exactly do

next(our great problem nearly solved)
we dare adorn the whole
with a distinct grandiloquent
deep D;while all skies fall

at last perfection,now and here
—but look:not sunlight?yes!
and(plunging rapturously up)
we spill our masterpiece

53

mighty guest of merely me

—traveller from eternity;
in a single wish,receive
all i am and dream and have.

Be thou gay by dark and day:
gay as only truth is gay
(nothing's false,in earth in air
in water and in fire,but fear—

mind's a coward;lies are laws)
laugh,and make each no thy yes:
love;and give because the why

—gracious wanderer,be thou gay

54

maybe god

is a child
's hand)very carefully
bring
-ing
to you and to
me(and quite with
out crushing)the

papery weightless diminutive

world
with a hole in
it out
of which demons with wings would be streaming if
something had(maybe they couldn't
agree)not happened(and floatingly int

o

55

(fea
therr
ain

:dreamin
g field o
ver forest &;

wh
o could
be

so
!f!
te

r?n
oo
ne)

56

a like a
grey
rock wanderin

g
through
pasture
worn

an creature whom
than
earth hers

elf
could
silent more no
be

57

(im)c-a-t(mo)
b,i;l:e

FallleA
ps!fl
OattumblI

sh?dr
IftwhirlF
(Ul)(lY)
&&&

away wanders:exact
ly;as if
not
hing had,ever happ
ene

D

58

after screamgroa
ning.ish:ly;
come

      (s

gruntsqueak
,while,
idling-is-grindstone

one;what:of.thumb

stutt(er(s a)mu)ddied
bushscytheblade
"pud-dih-gud"

)S

creang
roami
ngis

59

the little horse is newlY

Born)he knows nothing,and feels
everything;all around whom is

perfectly a strange
ness Of sun
light and of fragrance and of

Singing)is ev
erywhere(a welcom
ing dream:is amazing)
a worlD.and in

this world lies:smoothbeautifuL
ly folded;a(brea
thing and a gro

Wing)silence,who;
is:somE

oNe.

60

(nothing whichful about

thick big this
friendly
himself of
a boulder)nothing

mean in tenderly

whoms
of sizeless a
silence by noises
called people called

sunlight

(elsewhere flat the mechanical
itmaking
sickness of mind sprawls)
here

a livingly free mysterious

dreamsoul floatstands
oak by birch by maple
pine
by hemlock spruce by

tamarack(

nothing pampered puny
impatient
and nothing
ignoble

)everywhere wonder

6 1

if(touched by love's own secret)we,like homing
through welcoming sweet miracles of air
(and joyfully all truths of wing resuming)
selves,into infinite tomorrow steer

—souls under whom flow(mountain valley forest)
a million wheres which never may become
one(wholly strange;familiar wholly)dearest
more than reality of more than dream—

how should contented fools of fact envision
the mystery of freedom?yet,among
their loud exactitudes of imprecision,
you'll(silently alighting)and i'll sing

while at us very deafly a must stares
colossal hoax of clocks and calendars

62

in

Spring comes(no-
one
asks his name)

a mender
of things

with eager
fingers(with
patient
eyes)re

-new-

ing remaking what
other
-wise we should
have
thrown a-

way(and whose

brook
-bright flower-
soft bird
-quick voice loves

children
and sunlight and

mountains)in april(but
if he should
Smile)comes

nobody'll know

6 3

honour corruption villainy holiness
riding in fragrance of sunlight(side by side
all in a singing wonder of blossoming yes
riding)to him who died that death should be dead

humblest and proudest eagerly wandering
(equally all alive in miraculous day)
merrily moving through sweet forgiveness of spring
(over the under the gift of the earth of the sky

knight and ploughman pardoner wife and nun
merchant frere clerk somnour miller and reve
and geoffrey and all)come up from the never of when
come into the now of forever come riding alive

down while crylessly drifting through vast most
nothing's own nothing children go of dust

6 4

the of an it ignoblest he
to nowhere from arrive
human the most catastrophe
april might make alive

filthy some past imagining
whowhich of mad rags strode
earth ignorantly blossoming
a scarecrow demongod

countless in hatred pity fear
each more exactly than
the other un good people stare
for it or he is one

65

i thank You God for most this amazing
day:for the leaping greenly spirits of trees
and a blue true dream of sky;and for everything
which is natural which is infinite which is yes

(i who have died am alive again today,
and this is the sun's birthday;this is the birth
day of life and of love and wings:and of the gay
great happening illimitably earth)

how should tasting touching hearing seeing
breathing any—lifted from the no
of all nothing—human merely being
doubt unimaginable You?

(now the ears of my ears awake and
now the eyes of my eyes are opened)

66

the great advantage of being alive
(instead of undying)is not so much
that mind no more can disprove than prove
what heart may feel and soul may touch
—the great(my darling)happens to be
that love are in we,that love are in we

and here is a secret they never will share
for whom create is less than have
or one times one than when times where—
that we are in love,that we are in love:
with us they've nothing times nothing to do
(for love are in we am in i are in you)

this world(as timorous itsters all
to call their cowardice quite agree)
shall never discover our touch and feel
—for love are in we are in love are in we;
for you are and i am and we are(above
and under all possible worlds)in love

a billion brains may coax undeath
from fancied fact and spaceful time—
no heart can leap,no soul can breathe
but by the sizeless truth of a dream
whose sleep is the sky and the earth and the sea.
For love are in you am in i are in we

67

when faces called flowers float out of the ground
and breathing is wishing and wishing is having—
but keeping is downward and doubting and never
—it's april(yes,april;my darling)it's spring!
yes the pretty birds frolic as spry as can fly
yes the little fish gambol as glad as can be
(yes the mountains are dancing together)

when every leaf opens without any sound
and wishing is having and having is giving—
but keeping is doting and nothing and nonsense
—alive;we're alive,dear:it's(kiss me now)spring!
now the pretty birds hover so she and so he
now the little fish quiver so you and so i
(now the mountains are dancing,the mountains)

when more than was lost has been found has been found
and having is giving and giving is living—
but keeping is darkness and winter and cringing
—it's spring(all our night becomes day)o,it's spring!
all the pretty birds dive to the heart of the sky
all the little fish climb through the mind of the sea
(all the mountains are dancing;are dancing)

68

love our so right
is,all(each thing
most lovely)sweet
things cannot spring
but we be they'll

some or if where
shall breathe a new
(silverly rare
goldenly so)
moon,she is you

nothing may,quite
your my(my your
and)self without,
completely dare
be beautiful

one if should sing
(at yes of day)
younger than young
bird first for joy,
he's i he's i

69

now all the fingers of this tree(darling)have
hands,and all the hands have people;and
more each particular person is(my love)
alive than every world can understand

and now you are and i am now and we're
a mystery which will never happen again,
a miracle which has never happened before—
and shining this our now must come to then

our then shall be some darkness during which
fingers are without hands;and i have no
you:and all trees are(any more than each
leafless)its silent in forevering snow

—but never fear(my own,my beautiful
my blossoming)for also then's until

7 0

blue the triangular why

of a dream(with
crazily
eyes of window)may

be un

less it
were(floati
ng through

never)a kite

like face of
the child who's
every

child(&

therefore invisible)anyhow you
've(whoever
we are)stepped carefully o

ver(& i)some

newer
than life(or than
death)is on

f

ilthi
es
t

sidewalk blossoming glory

7 1

luminous tendril of celestial wish

(whying diminutive bright deathlessness
to these my not themselves believing eyes
adventuring,enormous nowhere from)

querying affirmation;virginal

immediacy of precision:more
and perfectly more most ethereal
silence through twilight's mystery made flesh—

dreamslender exquisite white firstful flame

—new moon!as(by the miracle of your
sweet innocence refuted)clumsy some
dull cowardice called a world vanishes,

teach disappearing also me the keen
illimitable secret of begin